Fight:
Win from Within

Fight:
Win from Within

Thomas Manning

IngramSpark | La Vergne, TN

FIGHT: WIN FROM WITHIN

Copyright © 2024 IngramSpark. All rights reserved. Except for brief quotations in critical publications or reviews, no part of this book may be reproduced in any manner without prior written permission from the publisher. Write: Permissions. One Ingram Blvd., La Vergne, TN 37086.

ISBN 13: 979-8-218-59154-0

Cataloguing-in-Publication Data

Fight: Win from Within by Thomas Manning.

xvi + 90 p.; 23 cm. Includes bibliographical references.
ISBN 13: 979-8-218-59154-0
I. Manning, Thomas. II. Fight: Win from Within.

CALL NUMBER 2024

Manufactured in the U.S.A.   2024

All Scripture quotations, unless otherwise indicated, are taken from the New International Version Bible (NIV), copyright 1972, 1978, 1984, 2011 by Biblica, Inc.TM Used by permission. All rights reserved.

Cover Design: Steven Da Silva

Dedication

I dedicate this book to my parents, Ed and Donna Manning, who lived the principles of this book before me when I was a young man. Their spiritual guidance, faithfulness to ministry, and sacrifice taught me to fight the spiritual fight, to depend on the Holy Spirit, and to overcome the attacks of the enemy and the temptations of the soul. Thank you for the foundation you laid in my life, which has enabled me to build upon it
for the glory of God.

Contents

Acknowledgments ix

S.O.A.P. DEVOTIONAL METHOD xi

Introduction xiii

Chapter 1 Fight: A Battle Within 1

Chapter 2 Led by the Spirit 9

Chapter 3 God Replacements 13

Chapter 4 Staying Pure 25

Chapter 5 Stages of Temptation 33

Chapter 6 Unity of the Church 43

Chapter 7 Growing in Unity 51

Chapter 8 The Deceitfulness of Selfish Ambition 57

Chapter 9 Humility 65

Chapter 10 The Battle of Envy 69

Chapter 11 How to Be Content 77

Conclusion More Than Conquerors 83

About the Author 85

Acknowledgments

Fight: Win from Within began as a spiritual growth campaign at Christian Life Center in South Florida. For six weeks, the church along with its small groups, daily devotions, kids, youth, and youth adults all aligned for a deeper study of Galatians 5. It was an exciting study for us as a church.

The topics covered in the companion guide include:

- Flesh vs. Spirit
- Idolatry vs. Love
- Impurity vs. Goodness, Faithfulness, and Self-Control
- Disunity vs. Peace and Patience
- Selfish Ambition vs. Kindness and Gentleness
- Envy vs. Joy

The companion study guide consists of forty-day devotions and life group discussions that provide an in-depth look at the fruit of the Spirit. I encourage you to pick up a copy of the companion guide.

This book represents the weekend services and the messages presented to the congregation.

So many have been involved in the development of the spiritual growth campaign: Pastor Kristian Reyes led the team of CLC Pastors: Kevin Richelieu, Steven Chapman, and Alex Omole. This team helped to map out the entire campaign.

Rebecca Chacon helped to write the companion guide, and CLC pastors and staff all helped to write the daily devotions. Andrew Scott help to edit and proof the companion guide.

Steven DaSilva and Bradley Reyes did all the graphic designs, including the cover.

Jennifer Thompson turned the sermons into chapters. Thank you for your diligence and heart to bring out the messages in a way that a reader could understand. Lois Olena edited and formatted the document.

Thank you to our wonderful congregation—Christian Life Center—without whom there would be no book. Your hunger for God's Word, your heart to serve, and your passion to reach the lost inspires me daily. I love the journey we are on with you. Candi and I love you, and we love our church!!

As a team, we present to you *Fight: Win from Within*.

S.O.A.P. DEVOTIONAL METHOD

One way to discover and apply God's principles to everyday life is for you and your family to use the SOAP method to think about what God is telling you. This acronym stands for:

S – Scripture – We recommend a systematic approach to Bible reading. For example, reading through one book at a time, or through the New Testament. If using a devotion, read each day or week.

O – Observation – What is God saying to you? What do you see? What was the author telling the audience? What is the passage about? If there are any words that stand out, look them up, study them, use another reference to get an overview of the passage. We call that the *rhema* word, the fresh word, the word God would have for you, in your walk in your journey, in your fight, right now.

A – Application – How do you apply this truth/passage to your life? Are there any areas in your life that do not align with the Scripture where you need to make changes? When you begin to write that application out, you're beginning to speak to yourself, you're making declarations, and you're beginning to determine in your will and your spirit that this is how you will walk it out and live it out.

P – Prayer – Take some time to pray about what God has revealed to you in this time through His Word, your observations, and the application of God's Word for your life. Ask the Lord how you can implement a given verse to your life. Commit to the Lord to do just that. Dedicate yourself to God, cleanse your heart, and cleanse your life. In that moment of prayer, you're making commitments to Him. Soak in it every day—whether five minutes or an hour. Whatever depth you want to go, you can do that in just a few moments. The key is do it *every day*, and let God speak through that time.

Introduction

In the quiet recesses of our hearts, a battle rages on—a battle as old as humanity itself that transcends the boundaries of time and culture. It is a battle fought not with swords and shields but with thoughts, emotions, desires, and decisions. It is a battle not against flesh and blood but against unseen forces that seek to undermine our very souls. This is the spiritual fight we face—the battle within.

In the pages of this book, we embark on a journey into the depths of our souls, into the unseen realm where the enemy of our souls wages war against us. This battle often goes unnoticed, hidden beneath the surface of our everyday lives. Yet, this battle shapes our thoughts, influences our choices, and determines our destinies.

The Apostle Paul, writing to the Ephesian Church, declares, "For we do not wrestle against flesh and blood, but against the rulers, against the authorities, against the cosmic powers over this present darkness, against the spiritual forces of evil in the heavenly places" (Eph 6:12, ESV).[1] These words remind us that our struggle is not merely against earthly adversaries but against a spiritual adversary who seeks to steal, kill, and destroy (John 10:10).

As we delve into this exploration of the spiritual fight, we will uncover the strategies and tactics of the enemy of our souls. We will discover the weapons we possess to stand firm in the battle and the armor we need to protect our hearts and minds. We will confront

---

[1] All Scripture quotations, unless otherwise noted, are from the New International Version.

the lies the enemy whispers in our ears and will learn how to replace them with the truth that sets us free.

But this is not merely a book about the enemy's schemes; it is a book about victory. It is about finding hope amid despair, courage in the face of fear, and strength in our weakness. It is about discovering the power of God's love, grace, and truth to transform our lives from the inside out.

This is not merely a book about the enemy's schemes; it is a book about victory.

In the chapters that follow, we will journey together through the battleground of the mind, the heart, and the will. We will explore the battlegrounds of temptation, doubt, and spiritual apathy. And we will emerge from this journey equipped, empowered, and emboldened to face the spiritual fight with confidence and resolve.

So, dear reader, whether you are well-acquainted with the battle within or just beginning to recognize its presence, this book is for you. It invites you to join the ranks of spiritual warriors who have gone before us, to take up the armor of God, and to stand firm in the fight for your soul. It is a call to embrace the truth that, in Christ, victory is not only possible but assured.

As we embark on this journey together, may you find renewed strength, deeper understanding, and a greater sense of purpose in the spiritual fight that rages on. May you discover the indomitable power of the One who fights alongside you, the One who has already secured the ultimate victory. For amid the battle within, there is hope, healing, and a path to triumph.

Fight: Win from Within

First Peter 5:8 reminds us of the urgent need to remain sober-minded and watchful in our spiritual journey. The Apostle Peter uses a vivid image of a roaring lion prowling, seeking to devour its prey. This verse serves as a sobering wake-up call, urging us to recognize that we are not passive observers in the spiritual battle but active participants. The devil, our adversary, is relentless in his pursuit to undermine our faith, disrupt our peace, and destroy our lives. However, in embracing sobriety and vigilance, we equip ourselves with the awareness and discernment needed to resist his schemes and to stand firm in the strength of our Savior, Jesus Christ. In the pages of this book, we will delve into the practical implications of this verse, exploring how we can stay alert, grounded in faith, and protected from the enemy's schemes in the ongoing battle for our souls.

Welcome to *Fight: Win from Within*.

Chapter 1

Fight: A Battle Within

As believers, we fight an invisible war; it comes at us in three different directions as three different battles. The first battle, which all believers fight, is **the battle against the enemy of your soul**, who is out to kill, steal, and destroy. Satan, the devil himself, is your infernal foe. He is out to destroy the work and plans of God and keep you in spiritual darkness. The Bible says that the enemy of your soul has blinded you to the truth of God's Word. He tries to steal the Word of God from your life and to keep you in doubt, fear, and confusion. He tries to keep your life in chaos, to steal your peace, and to derail the work of God. Your infernal foe, Satan himself, tries to do everything he can to get you to step out of the will of God, turn your back on Him, and doubt the plans and purpose He has for your life. He will tempt you, and if you give in to that temptation, that sin will separate you from Him. Temptation itself is not sin. However, when I do not discipline my desires and I *give in* to temptation, that sin brings separation between God and me. Temptation will get you to turn away from the truth; Satan will entice you, lay bait out to you, and get your eyes focused on the cares of this world. He will use deceit and come at your marriage, children, and family. The enemy of your soul does everything he can to get you to turn away from God.

The second battle believers will face is what's called **the battle of this world**, or the external foe. It involves the systems of this world, the values of this world we live in, and the philosophies of thought that are influenced by the enemy of your soul. Through these avenues, people around you will mock you and ridicule you. They will get you to a place where you start questioning your belief and what you've come to know is true and right in the Word of God. The values of this world entice us, and in those values, we begin to turn away from God himself. That is why Paul says in Romans 12:2 not to be conformed to this world. He's talking about the values, philosophies, and ways or systems of this world. When we discuss what's happening around us, these are what he is referring to. Politics, wars, and conflict are part of that. So is racism, prejudice, and injustice—any values in the ways of the world that the enemy can use to influence your soul work hand in hand with him, going after your heart. Throughout 1 and 2 Timothy, Paul says to Timothy, the young preacher who would be leading a congregation, that the fight is intensifying.

In the last several years, I have felt this intensity rise. The world and its values are trying to break apart churches and believers and bring disunity and dissension in order to squeeze us into the mold of the world. The values, philosophies, and systems of the world are influenced by the enemy of your soul.

The best way to fight back is through spiritual warfare. The problem is that too many believers, especially Pentecostal believers, think that spiritual warfare is just something we do at a prayer meeting. They think it means just going to a church service and making some declarations. But spiritual warfare used against the enemy of our soul involves a lifestyle, not just an occasional event of rebuking the enemy or casting out demons.

The third and greatest battle we fight is **the battle within**. This is the flesh, our internal foe. Sometimes we blame the devil, and sometimes we blame the world. However, this is a separate battle. The flesh is a fruit killer because it does not want the fruit of the Spirit to grow.

There is a story about the famous preacher, Charles Spurgeon, who trained many preachers. One day he was sitting with his assistant, and a young man got up to talk about the armor of God. As he spoke, he put on actual armor. After this young preacher had all the armor on, he asked where the enemy was. Charles Spurgeon replied, "He's within you." You are the fighter in the pursuit of the Lord.

Paul is transparent about this battle with the flesh in a couple places in Scripture: Galatians 5, Romans 7, and Romans and 8. In Galatians, he says, "So I say, walk by the Spirit, and you will not gratify the desires of the flesh. For the flesh desires what is contrary to the Spirit, and the Spirit what is contrary to the flesh. They are in conflict with each other, so that you are not to do whatever you want" (Gal 5:16-17).

The Definition of the Flesh

The *flesh* is the sinful nature, made up of your carnal (sensuous) person and its desires. This includes old patterns of your unredeemed humanity. One who has been regenerated (saved) differs from someone who has yet to be saved (unregenerated). This difference is reflected in their thinking, way of life, and destination.

The fight is with our carnal or fleshly person. When you continue to live by these old patterns, the Bible calls that "walking in the flesh" because you're living under the control of your unredeemed habits. The Apostle Paul in Romans 7 describes the civil war within as a constant fight:

> And I know that nothing good lives in me, that is, in my sinful nature. I want to do what is right, but I can't. I want to do what is good, but I don't. I don't want to do what is wrong, but I do it anyway. But if I do what I don't want to do, I am not really the one doing wrong; it is sin living in me that does it. I have discovered this principle of life—that when I want to do what is right, I inevitably do what is

wrong. I love God's law with all my heart. But there is another power within me that is at war with my mind. This power makes me a slave to the sin that is still within me. Oh, what a miserable person I am! Who will free me from this life that is dominated by sin and death? Thank God! The answer is in Jesus Christ our Lord. So you see how it is: In my mind I really want to obey God's law, but because of my sinful nature I am a slave to sin (Rom 7:18-25, NLT).

When we let our carnal person rule, our focus is on self. Just as a toddler learning to walk starts to depend on their legs, when they stand up, those legs are wobbly. Even so, they depend on those legs to carry them, move them, and hold them up. They have a destination they're trying to get to. They will keep going so that there is consistent movement.

Do not walk according to the flesh.

When you walk after the flesh, you place your dependence on self-sufficiency to take you where you want to go (your needs), instead of letting God rule over your life. The primary characteristic of the sinful nature is that it is always trying to please itself—living for self, doing what self thinks is best.

Question: *Is it possible for one living for God to walk in the flesh?*

Outwardly, one can appear to be living for God but inwardly be indulging in the sinful nature. Galatians says that God rejects the efforts of people trying to do things their own way. He refers to Abraham and Sarah and how they concocted their own plan on how to fulfill the promise of God for a son. Ishmael is referred to as a "son of the flesh" who God rejected. Sarah and Abraham did not think that God could do what He had promised. When you use the flesh, and therefore reject God, God will reject the product of what comes from that. Our self-effort, in God's eyes, doesn't count.

The Desire of the Flesh

As Paul writes to the church in Rome, he says, "There is therefore now no condemnation for those who are in Christ Jesus" (Rom 8:1, NKJV).

Many people in churches today say they are "in Christ" but still walk after the patterns of the flesh because they have not learned to win from within. There is a fight, and they do not even realize how to win it. The evidence that you are truly in Christ is that there is no condemnation because you will not walk according to the flesh but by the Spirit. For the law of the Spirit is life in Christ Jesus, who made you free from the law of sin and death. We are born into the nature of Adam (Rom 5) who along with Eve disobeyed God (Gen 3) and walked according to the flesh. Therefore, because we are born into this predisposition to follow the works of the flesh, there is a battle. But when you give your life to Christ, you have victory because He made you free from the law of sin and death. The works of the flesh could not give you freedom. God intervened on your behalf by sending His Son. This is the redemptive work of Christ fulfilled in you. You are made righteous through Christ's righteousness when you accept Him as your Savior, as Paul describes in Romans 8:

> For those who live according to the flesh set their minds on the things of the flesh, but those who live according to the Spirit, the things of the Spirit. For to be carnally minded is death, but to be spiritually minded is life and peace (vv. 5-6, NKJV).

The Spirit gives life and peace. It is not automatic. The flesh wants to kill the life and peace of God's Spirit. If the flesh wins, spiritual death occurs and kills the fruit. You cannot walk in both at the same time.

This situation is like football. On the field at any one time, you have an offense and a defense. They have different goals. Spiritually, the Spirit wants you to move in life, in peace, and in the purpose of God, but there is a defense trying to stop the offense from moving. In your life, the defense is the works of the flesh. It's the carnal nature, the flesh in opposition to the Spirit. If your spiritual progress is being blocked, that is a sign that the enemy is trying to block you and that you are in this conflict of the flesh and the spirit.

As believers we must remain unified and encourage one another. Every person is caught in this battle. We must stay determined to be victorious, as Paul says in Galatians 5,

> So I say, let the Holy Spirit guide your lives. Then you won't be doing what your sinful nature craves. The sinful nature wants to do evil, which is just the opposite of what the Spirit wants. And the Spirit gives us desires that are the opposite of what the sinful nature desires. These two forces are constantly fighting each other, so you are not free to carry out your good intentions (vv. 16-17, NLT).

This is the fight. The question often asked is, "How do you know if you are walking according to the flesh?"

Paul answers this question as he continues in Galatians 5,

> When you follow the desires of your sinful nature, the results are very clear: idolatry and witchcraft; hatred, discord, jealousy, fits of rage, selfish ambition, dissensions, factions and envy; drunkenness, orgies, and the like. I warn you, as I did before, that those who live like this will not inherit the kingdom of God (vv. 19-20, NLT).

Paul says *will* fight this battle within, and it is a battle in the category of your **morality**. When you give in to sinful desires, sexual impurity, lustful pleasures, immorality, adultery, and homosexuality, you are walking after the flesh and not the spirit.

The second category Paul begins to talk about has to do with **your faith or religion**. He addresses idolatry—worshiping something and putting it above God, making it a priority. I have seen so many things become an idol: sports, careers, and education. I have even watched people put their families in a place that it becomes idolatry, and they quit following God because of their family. When that idolatry happens, suddenly your faith begins to shift.

The third category is a list of things **socially**. You may have hostility toward another person or always be quarreling or disruptive. Maybe you're always cursing, always just saying things that result in fights, or never seem to get along with anybody. You have selfish ambition. You gossip or talk about someone to another person who is neither a part of the problem nor part of the solution. You envy and have jealousy. All these things lead to disunity in the body of Christ. These are the works of the flesh Paul refers to in Galatians 5:20.

The flesh wants to stop you from growing in Christ. We need to get rid of the negative habits or behavior that steal our time and attention. How do we overcome the flesh? As believers in God, we can overcome through the power of the Spirit.

In Romans 8, Paul helps us understand how this happens:

> So letting your sinful nature control your mind leads to death. But letting the Spirit control your mind leads to life and peace. For the sinful nature is always hostile to God. It never did obey God's laws, and it never will. That's why those who are still under the control of their sinful nature can never please God (vv. 6-8, NLT).

Fight: Win from Within

Chapter 2

Led by the Spirit

> But you are not controlled by your sinful nature. You are controlled by the Spirit if you have the Spirit of God living in you. (And remember that those who do not have the Spirit of Christ living in them do not belong to him at all.) And Christ lives within you, so even though your body will die because of sin, the Spirit gives you life because you have been made right with God. The Spirit of God, who raised Jesus from the dead, lives in you. And just as God raised Christ Jesus from the dead, he will give life to your mortal bodies by this same Spirit living within you. Therefore, dear brothers and sisters, you have no obligation to do what your sinful nature urges you to do (Rom 8:9-12, NLT).

We must take on the defense by walking in the Spirit so we can begin to see that there is victory and strength. Galatians 5 contrasts what's going on; if we have crucified the sinful nature, then in that we also crucify its passions and desires. This means we can live by the Spirit and keep in step with the Spirit. There is a process and a progression that takes place.

Too many people go after the things of the flesh and try to overcome them. Paul says, "Listen, the order is wrong. You walk in the Spirit, and you *will* overcome the works of the flesh." When you walk toward the things of God, the work of God, the purpose of God, and the plan of God, you're walking by the Spirit. You defeat the flesh. You can win from within by being Spirit filled. Being filled with the Spirit is where the Holy Spirit now takes control.

The Spirit's power comes as we seek God's infilling and seek to know Him in a deeper way and to glorify Him.

> "Since we live by the Spirit, let us keep in step with the Spirit" (Gal 5:25)

Being led by the Spirit means to be filled in such a way that we're controlled by the Spirit. We need to learn how to get fully immersed in the presence of God, which will allow us to overcome the works of the flesh. Our character needs to come into alignment with the Spirit of God.

By being sensitive to the voice of the Spirit, He will guide you in a variety of ways. As the Spirit directs us, we need to respond. This begins with cleansing our hearts. During this process we learn to believe and seek God. As we grow, we surrender our heart to God. This is the starting point.

In my life, I receive the empowerment of the Spirit by seeking the Spirit of God. I even receive what's called a "prayer language." I receive an ability to commune with God, and as I commune with God in my prayer language, that strengthens my inner man as I'm being filled by the Spirit.

When I am filled with the Spirit, I can then allow the Holy Spirit to lead me, as directed in Galatians 5:16. I am thus empowered and strengthened. The Holy Spirit now begins to guide me and lead me. He helps me to walk and be what God wants me to be. For my life, being Spirit-led means that the Spirit is in control of my life. I focus on the ministry of Christ and the mission of Christ, which starves my flesh and feeds my spirit. As I do that, I deny the works of the flesh, and my "spirit man" comes alive. When I'm controlled by the Spirit, I am praying, reading the Word, worshipping at home and in church, discussing the Word of God, and getting together with other believers who encourage me. Every one of these is a punch to the works of the flesh. I do not feed the works of the flesh anymore. Rather, I flee them. When I do, I can live as an overcomer in Christ. This is a spiritual fight. The Holy Spirit will give you the power to move forward as you feed your spirit.

> Jesus replied: "'Love the Lord your God with all your heart and with all your soul and with all your mind.' This is the first and greatest commandment"
> (Matt 22:37-38, NIV).

It's our choice. Ask yourself the following questions:

- Am I going *all in*?
- Do I want to go deeper?
- Am I going to follow God's plan for my life to fulfill my purpose?
- Am I allowing Him to anoint and empower me?

When you say yes to these questions, you give God control, and transformation happens as you press into Him and get out of the way.

As a result, the fruit of the Spirit is planted and can begin to grow in you. Galatians 5:22 describes that fruit: "But the fruit of the Spirit is love, joy, peace, patience, kindness, goodness, faithfulness, gentleness, and self-control."

I must put the fruit of the Spirit on; it does not happen automatically. I must begin to live a life walking after the Spirit. As I put on more of the fruit of the Spirit, I learn how to live with joy and how to live a life of patience, kindness, goodness, faithfulness, gentleness, and self-control. Carnality leads to living out the works of the flesh, but when I am led by the Spirit, that leads to putting on the fruit of the Spirit.

When we put on the fruit of the Spirit, we take on the image of Christ. This is called being "in Christ," or having the nature of Christ and being in the likeness of God. This spiritual battle is the fight, and it's a battle within.

Chapter 3

God Replacements

The enemy manipulates and works in our weaknesses to awaken desires that lead us to sin. If he can make us discontent, then we will try to fill a void with things that God calls the "desires of your sinful nature." Only God can give us peace, but we try to fill any void in our hearts with what the Bible calls "the works of the flesh."

Paul says this in Galatians 5:19-20, 24:

> When you follow the desires of your sinful nature, THE RESULTS are very clear: idolatry and witchcraft; hatred, discord, jealousy, fits of rage, selfish ambition, dissensions, factions … Those who belong to Christ Jesus have crucified the sinful nature with its passions and desires. Since we live by the Spirit, let us keep in step with the Spirit (NLT).

This is the great battle, and this battle is *within*. It is the fight of our carnal nature with the work of the Spirit.

The Definition of Idolatry

Scripture contains thousands of references to idolatry. We don't seem to give them much thought, as though they are obsolete. When we think about idolatry or idol worship, we picture bowing to an idol—to some carved statue or a pagan god. We think of far-away places where natives might be dancing around a huge fire.

When my wife and I were missionaries in Vienna, Austria, I was walking the grounds of the United Nations one day. As I was praying, I walked by a gentleman standing in front of a tree, worshipping it, just like as we worship Jehovah God. He believed that tree would save him or help him in his needs.

It can be easy to think that idolatry is not an issue for today. However, it is all through the Word of God and one of the main themes of Scripture in both the Old and New Testaments.

Paul refers to it in Colossians 3:5 (NLT): "So put to death the sinful, earthly things lurking within you. Have nothing to do with sexual immorality, impurity, lust, and evil desires. Don't be greedy, for a greedy person is an **idolater**, worshiping the things of this world."

What is idolatry? There are two parts to it biblically. The first part of idolatry is the idol itself—a statue or image of a false god. The second part has to do with the people bowing to and worshipping an idol. Idol worship was forbidden by God all through Scripture. As these two parts come together, it means people giving devotion or sharing the essence of their love toward an object. When we link the devotion to something or someone, we begin to step into the realm of idolatry. For example, we may give our complete and undivided attention, devotion, passion, love, or commitment to a person, project, or object other than God. We step into this realm of idolatry when something or someone begins to absorb our heart and imagination more than God. Whatever has our attention may even begin to take first place within our heart, where it becomes an idol.

Idolatry occurs when someone dedicates their full attention, devotion, passion, love, or commitment to a person, project, or object instead of God. When anything other than God becomes the foremost priority in one's mind, they have, to some extent, fallen into the sin of idolatry.

The Apostle John warned against allowing this to happen: "Dear children, keep away from anything that might take God's place in your hearts" (1 John 5:21, TLB).

The biggest struggle in overcoming this battle is that people don't understand and identify the gods or idols that may be entrapping them, getting them to a place where that thing takes a priority that only God wants in our lives. We find ourselves in a place we shouldn't be. It's not that some of these things are wrong or immoral. They're amoral or morally neutral. But when God is no longer the priority, then that thing has become a priority.

What is replacing God in your heart or life?

What is replacing God in your heart or life? What is taking the place God desires and should take, which we may not even be aware a God replacement is taking place? The challenge for all of us is to ask ourselves, "Where have I allowed God replacements to take place?"

We must challenge any God replacement taking the place, trying to come into a part of our hearts that only God wants. Dwight Moody, the great preacher says, "You don't have to go to heathen lands today to find false gods. America is full of them. Whatever you love more than God is your idol."[1]

The Apostle Paul says in 1 Corinthians 10:13-14,

> No temptation has seized you except what is common to man. And God is faithful; he will not let you be tempted beyond what you can bear. But when you are tempted, he will also provide a way out so that you can stand up under

---

[1] Dwight Moody, quoted in George Sweeting, *Who Said That?* (Chicago: Moody Publishers, 1995), 270.

it. Therefore, my dear friends, flee from idolatry (1 Cor 10:13-14).

The command against idol worship is one of the Ten Commandments given in the Book of Exodus. When the Ten Commandments were given, Moses was up on the mountain with God. But down in the valley, the Israelites were already building themselves an idol to worship, trusting in an idol they had come to know more than trusting in God. One of the very commandments God was giving to Moses warned against that very idolatrous behavior:

> You must not make for yourself an idol of any kind or an image of anything in the heavens or on the earth or in the sea. You must not bow down to them or worship them, for I, the LORD your God, am a jealous God who will not tolerate your affection for any other gods. I lay the sins of the parents upon their children; the entire family is affected—even children in the third and fourth generations of those who reject me (Exod 20:4-5, NLT).

What things are we putting before God today? It could be our identity or image—worrying about what people think of us or what they see in us. Are we driven by the image we portray? If we are, how does it manifest itself in the way we look, in what we post, and in what we do to get the approval of others?

Could the thing we are putting before God be our money? We think gaining money just has to do with making a living and preparing ourselves for the future, but has a root grown into our heart where money has become an idol in our life?

For many, entertainment has become an idol. Some people spend hours watching TV/videos or movies but cannot find ten minutes to pray.

Sometimes idolatry can result from trying to fill a void due to wanting to be accepted. The urges and desires of our flesh can result in our sexuality leading us out of our comfort zone. We want to control things and not allow dependency on what God wants to do to control our comfort.

Finally, what about our phones? There's an app that tells us how much we use our phone, how much we pick it up, and monitors the time we spend looking at different things. We can tell by reviewing data if our devotion to our phone has gotten out of hand!

None of these behaviors are wrong by themselves, but when we put too much of our focus on them, we need to be aware that these may have the potential to take the place of God in our lives. They may not be something we say we're *worshiping*, yet upon closer look, if we're honest, we may see these things have taken first place in our lives. The battle rages on for our heart.

The Battle for Your Heart!

Biblically, the heart is a metaphor for the center or core of a person. It is the spiritual hub, and your life flows from the heart. It makes up your personality, motives, emotions, and your will. It is your true identity.

Proverbs describes the role of the heart: "As a face is reflected in water, so the heart reflects the real person" (27:19, NLT).

This is why God is described as a *jealous* God. He wants nothing competing for the throne of your heart, the top spot of your affection. This issue goes back to the Ten Commandments, where God showed over and over that He was a jealous or zealous God. He lavishly puts His consuming love for us on display, drawing us back into a redemptive relationship with Him because sin had broken that relationship. Therefore, He wants nothing to compete with the love He wants to pour out on us. His greatest desire, though, is that we love Him in return with a song that rises not just from our lips but from our hearts.

God's greatest desire is that we come to know His love and to understand that He loves us so much that He sent His Son Jesus to bring us back into right relationship with Him. That's why Christ gave His life. That is the core of our faith, that Christ gave His life willingly, was crucified on a cross, and rose from a grave to show that death had no victory. The grave could not hold Him down. Therefore, we are saved, made right with God, and redeemed. Our sin is no longer counted against us. We are now one with God, walking with Him.

Your heart defines and determines who you are, how you think, and what you do. Because everything flows from it, your heart is the frontline for the battle. Proverbs describes its important role: "Guard your heart above all else, for it determines the course of your life" (4:23, NLT).

Let's say one day you go for a hike. You come to this beautiful creek at the foot of the mountains, formed by streams coming down the mountain. As you're standing there to take in the beauty of that moment, you begin to see trash floating all around. As the trash fills up, you begin to wonder, *what is this trash doing here?* It appears that someone has dumped their trash from camping. Why would someone throw their trash in this beautiful creek? It begins to bother you, so you begin to pick up the trash to make it a beautiful place again. The trash keeps coming, and it takes you a couple hours to get it all cleaned up. Finally, you reach a point where you look out and it's a pretty sight again. You sit there longer enjoying the view and just taking it in. As you leave, you decide to go back again tomorrow and enjoy the beauty. You come back the next day to find there's more trash in the creek and in the spring that's there. Again, you wonder, *who would have dumped their trash last night into this creek?* You decide to investigate and begin to walk. As you're walking and going up toward the foot of the mountain, you come to a point where you realize what the problem is—this creek runs along next to a dump.

The back of the dump has given way, and trash is flowing into the creek. You could stay all day long in that area where there's a beautiful spring and the creek is flowing into it. But the problem is, the next day more trash is going to come. You would find yourself picking up trash every day.

You could go and clean the creek every day, but what's the point if it's going to keep flowing from the garbage dump? If you want the creek to be clean, you must fix the issue at the dump.

Your heart is the source from which your life flows.

Our heart is like that creek—the source of all life where everything flows. We can try to pick up the trash around that creek every day, not realizing there's a problem upstream. This is where most people stay in their Christian life. Most people stay picking up the trash around the creek. For example, they come to a worship service once a week or maybe twice a month or maybe once a month. The less they come, the more trash gets built up. When we come into a worship experience in person or online, in your private devotions, or whenever you're worshiping, you're getting rid of trash, and you're cleaning up around the creek. You're looking at the works of the flesh in the trash. What you have forgotten is that the source is your heart and that what you see comes from your heart. That's where everything begins to flow. It takes commitment to walk upstream and address the true source. If we ignore the heart, we'll never solve the issue.

The Problem is That Your Spirit is Fighting Alone

For many believers, their spirit is fighting, but their will has not engaged and continues to give in. It continues to give into the works of the flesh, and they find themselves going back to the throne, asking God for forgiveness. God says, "You're just picking up the trash around the creek. You've got to get back to the source of what is in the heart." Are there idols driving us that are dumping the trash into our life? If so, that's where we've got to start doing the work. Your spirit is fighting against the works of the flesh, but the source is the idolatry—the things you put above God. It's time to walk upstream and look deep within your heart. We do this by going through a self-evaluation. These are times of awareness when we can soak in prayer and in the presence of God.

This can take place during a time of worship, at church, or at home, when music is playing, or wherever you're soaking in the Lord. In that prayer, what you do in those moments, you're walking upstream. The more you go upstream, the more you get to the source of the problem, and the more you'll begin to see where the enemy is trying to awaken the works of the flesh. As you see where the enemy is working in your life, you can begin to get prepared for the attack and know that temptation is going to be the gateway to get you into that path of idolatry and the works of the flesh.

When I go through this process, I begin to prepare for the attack. In those times of prayer, soaking, seeking God, getting into the Word, and having my devotions, I ask Him to show me if there is anything taking priority in my life more than Him and His desire for my life. I begin to determine and make a commitment. There are no more excuses. I'm going to walk upstream and deal with these issues of the heart. I'm going to let God take the throne in my life.

Think of an MRI. You get an injection with some dye. The contrast medium enhances the image quality and allows the radiologist more accuracy and confidence in their diagnosis. In the same way, we can step back and evaluate what things have become more important than God.

God-Replacement Questions

Here are some questions that help reveal some problem areas:

1. **What do you think of more than anything else?** What consumes most of your thoughts? Is it your career, children, marriage, or popularity?

2. **What disappoints you?** When we feel overwhelmed by disappointment, it's a good sign that something has become far more important to us than it should be. It shows intense hope and longing on something other than God.

3. **What do you complain about the most?** Maybe ask someone close to you to answer that. Is it your financial situation, or lack of respect at work?

4. **Where do you make financial sacrifices?** Where you put your treasure, there your heart is also. Where your money goes shows what God is winning at in your heart. If a stranger looked at your checkbook or your budget, what priorities would they see?

5. **What do you worry about?** What would happen if you lost your job or someone in your life? We can care so deeply about something or someone that it has a hold on us deep inside. What wakes you up at night?

6. **Where or what is your sanctuary?** When you have a bad day, what do you do? Do you turn to comfort food, vent to a friend, or play video games? What is the emotional

rescue? When you're suffering, how do you respond? What do you do when your loved one has been diagnosed with some form of illness or your teenager or young adult is in an accident that puts them in a coma? What about when your spouse loses his or her job? Is God your sanctuary in the darkest fear and hours of life?

7. **What makes you angry or infuriates you?** Not being in control? A lack of patience?

8. **What are your dreams?** Are they God dreams, or personal dreams? Is your motivation to give God glory or are you motivated by your own glory or fame?

Take time to reflect, journal, and let the "dye" reveal if any **GOD-REPLACEMENT** has taken place.

How Do You Win the Battle for the Heart?

Learning to walk in the Spirit and crucify the flesh begins with recognizing anything becoming a **GOD-REPLACEMENT** in your life.

To overcome idolatry, Paul says must be Spirit-filled and Spirit-led. When the Spirit guides you, then you can crucify the works of the flesh. I encourage you as you to begin to look for and find God replacement issues—ask Holy Spirit to fill you and remove them from your life. Pray to be filled with wisdom and guidance and to remain sensitive to learn to walk in step with the Spirit. The Apostle Paul says that the Holy Spirit will guide your life; "Then," he says, "you won't be doing what your sinful nature craves" (Gal 5:16, NLT).

The second thing to overcome the battle is to let God take the throne of your heart by putting on the fruit of the Spirit. It's not enough to *know* the fruit. You've got to *put on* the fruit by *growing it in your life*. It's obvious when a person is driven by the flesh. Likewise, the work of the Spirit is also evident when a person is being led by the Spirit. They put on Christ and have the character or nature of Christ. They reflect the fruit of the Spirit.

"But the fruit of the Spirit is love, joy, peace, patience, kindness, goodness, faithfulness, gentleness and self-control" (Gal 5:22-23, NLT).

This is not just something just happens automatically but something you grow. It is the work of spiritual growth and maturity in your life. Too many believers just think this reflecting of the fruit of the Spirit will just happen instantaneously or automatically, but walking by the Spirit is a process of putting on the fruit of the Spirit.

The more we allow God to direct our steps and help us walk in obedience, the more we can overcome the flesh and live out His purpose.

Fight: Win from Within

Chapter 4

Staying Pure

> When you follow the desires of your sinful nature, the results are very clear: sexual immorality, impurity, lustful pleasures (Gal 5:19, NLT).

When we read what the Apostle Paul wrote to the Galatians in chapter 5 of his letter to them, we can hear the battle taking place in his words—a strong fight where the flesh draws us in and our cravings pull us along:

> So I say, let the Holy Spirit guide your lives. Then you won't be doing what your sinful nature craves. The sinful nature wants to do evil, which is just the opposite of what the Spirit wants. And the Spirit gives us desires that are the opposite of what the sinful nature desires. These two forces are constantly fighting each other, so you are not free to carry out your good intentions. But when you are directed by the Spirit, you are not under obligation to the law of Moses. When you follow the desires of your sinful nature, the results are very clear: sexual immorality, impurity, lustful pleasures (Gal 5:16-19, NLT)

Paul notes how the enemy stirs up the desires and the lustful passions within our heart. The flesh in itself is not sinful, but when we give in to the flesh, that is when we sin. The human body is created and given by God and for His use. It is not the body that is evil nor the flesh and blood that is evil. Through the desires of the heart and mind, though, where we get captivated by that which the enemy stirs within us—*that* pulls us down.

The Bible says we are the temple of the Holy Spirit who desires to dwell within us. When we worship, we empty ourselves of the works of the flesh and that has corroded the nature within us, so that the Holy Spirit can come and reside in His temple. If we allow sin to dwell within us, it will grow stronger all the time, for it originates in the heart. The sins of the flesh, listed in Galatians, are clearly seen throughout Scripture. Paul lists three things there that this chapter will address: sexual immorality, impurity, and lustful pleasures.

We live today in a culture obsessed with sexuality and the sensual. Sexual images are used to sell everything. It's the #1 value in our society. Studies show that three-quarters of cases of sexuality on TV involve illicit, pre-marital sex. Over a year, the average viewer will see over 9,000 sex acts or implied sexuality with 81 percent of them outside of marriage. By the time a child is eighteen, he or she will see over 93,000 scenes of sexual content, of which 72,000 are pre-marital or extra-marital in nature. Years ago, someone would have had to go to a specialty shop if they wanted to obtain pornography. Today it comes into the home through computers, talk shows, and even on our cell phones.

When we lived in Vienna, Austria, nudity and sexual content was very explicit. It would be on billboards and other places where the public could see it. One day one of our missionary colleagues (Papa Bill, in his seventies) was taking my four-year-old son to preschool when he heard Andrew chuckling and laughing in the backseat. Papa Bill realized that there was a billboard with a nude woman at the intersection where they had stopped. He asked Andrew why he was laughing. Andrew, in his innocence of that day, said "Papa Bill, she forgot to get dressed." That's how we used to feel about things we viewed; it would make us uncomfortable. The problem today is that many believers are getting desensitized to this immorality, and what used to make us uncomfortable doesn't anymore. What should make us turn a TV channel doesn't make us want to do that anymore because we are no longer shocked by what we see in society.

Paul tells the Thessalonians to "be holy and pure" and to "keep clear of all sexual sin" (immorality) because God "… has not called us to be dirty-minded and full of lust but to be holy and clean" (1 Thess 4:3, 7, TLB).

God's Plan for Sexuality

Sexuality is a gift from God.

The Book of Genesis describes sexuality as a gift from God:

> Then the Lord God caused the man to fall into a deep sleep, and took one of his ribs and closed up the place from which he had removed it, and made the rib into a woman, and brought her to the man. "This is it!" Adam exclaimed. "She is part of my own bone and flesh! Her name is 'woman' because she was taken out of a man." This explains why a man leaves his father and mother and is joined to his wife in such a way that the two become one person. Now although the man and his wife were both naked, neither of them was embarrassed or ashamed (2:21-25, TLB).

In Adam's reaction there was no guilt or shame. Genesis 2:25 says that although the man and his wife were both naked, neither of them was embarrassed or ashamed. There was no shame or condemnation for what God had created in sexuality. God created sexuality for a purpose. The enjoyment, the pleasure, and intimacy result in a spiritual bond between a husband and a wife. That's why Scripture says that "the two shall become one." Scripture also tells us that our sexuality is a gift from God for procreation and reproduction. We are to be fruitful and multiply and replenish the earth.

> We are no longer shocked by
> what we see in society.

The problem with sexual pleasure is that it can become an obsession that the enemy perverts and twists to get us to compromise. We attempt to have that enjoyment or fulfillment and that intimacy outside of the boundaries God has designed. As we buy into and adopt it, we find ourselves being pulled in.

How Do I Stay Pure?

To stay pure, we must adopt God's standard. Psalm 119:9 tells us that we keep our way pure by living according to the Word. Why do we get ourselves in a place where we walk in guilt, shame, and condemnation? We face consequences because we follow our own sinful nature and desires. God wants us to keep clear of all sexual sins. Sometimes we focus on certain sexual sins and overlook others. Galatians shows us that sexual sins include sexual immorality, impurity, and lustful pleas.

We must adopt God's standard. We must settle these questions:

1. Am I more committed to doing what God says will meet my needs or what I think will meet my needs?
2. Am I going to follow my Creator or what the culture tells me is acceptable?
3. Am I going to follow the Word, or the ways of the world?

I get to choose. God says that sex is something to be exclusive between a husband and wife in a committed marriage together.

God's standard has not changed. Society might say it has, but God's plan remains the same.

God has not changed His standard. Let's go back to Galatians 5 where Paul writes, "When you follow the desires of your sinful nature, the results are very clear: sexual immorality, impurity, lustful pleasures" (v. 19, NLT). The Word of God is clear: sex is for a husband and a wife in a marriage relationship only. Outside of those parameters, the Bible tells us it is wrong. Sexual immorality—lustful passions and desires—takes us down a lot of different roads. If you're married, and you find yourself having sex with somebody other than your spouse, the Bible calls that adultery. Sex with another person of the same sex is homosexuality. Incest is sex with someone in your family. Fornication is where two singles are having sexual relationships with one another, and living together outside of the bounds of marriage is considered immorality. All of these are sexual sins, and they are wrong. There are no lesser or greater sexual sins; this a thought contrary to the will and the purpose of God. Again, the Apostle Paul provides guidance on this when he writes,

> For God wants you to be holy and pure and to keep clear of all sexual sin so that each of you will marry in holiness and honor—not in lustful passion as the heathen do, in their ignorance of God and his ways. And this also is God's will: that you never cheat in this matter by taking another man's wife because the Lord will punish you terribly for this, as we have solemnly told you before. For God has not called us to be dirty-minded and full of lust but to be holy and clean. If anyone refuses to live by these rules, he is not disobeying the rules of men but of God who gives his Holy Spirit to you (1 Thess 4:3-8, TLB).

I have a question for those of you in a dating relationship and waiting years to get married. If you're truly in love, why are you waiting to get married? To singles in love, Paul says it's better to marry than to burn with lust. The marriage relationship has been established for life and for something beautiful. Sometimes, because we delay marriage, we idolize the kind of person we should marry. Since no one is perfect, we begin to discount people. We find ourselves delaying for a long time, but those urges and desires remain. It's fine if you feel you must delay, but you must discipline your desires.

> Sex is for a husband and wife
> in marriage only!

In his letter to the Thessalonians, Paul explains that when we commit any type of sexual sin, we willingly disobey. We act like unbelievers who don't have convictions. As a Christ follower, you must have convictions about your sexuality. Those convictions don't lead you to follow the passions of your flesh but lead you to cry out to God. My prayer and heartfelt cry are that you will desire to do God's will for your life and that you will want to be righteous and holy in His sight. You walk a road of purity because of the desire to honor Him and be all He wants you to be. We should act differently than unbelievers. His Word says that if we deny that, and act on those emotions and passions, then we are acting like unbelievers. As a result of that, the Word says, we will be judged. God created boundaries for our benefit and protection.

As I was driving yesterday trying to get to a certain place, there was a sign that said DO NOT ENTER. I was a little bit frustrated because now I would have to go all the way around again. But the sign was there to warn me of trouble ahead. It was for my protection, not to punish me. God says that our sexuality reflects that; it's not to punish us but to protect us.

The Reward

The reward for this obedience is that God will fulfill His purpose through you. As you walk in obedience to Him, He can use you. His promise is a conditional one: "If you keep yourself pure, you will be a utensil God can use for His purpose. Your life will be clean, and you will be ready for the Master to use you for every good work" (2 Tim 2:21, NLT).

The good news is that if you have struggled in this area, you can repent and ask for forgiveness, and God will restore you. Wholeness and freedom come as you walk in His way.

Fight: Win from Within

Chapter 5

Stages of Temptation

The way to stay pure involves understanding the stages of temptation. There is a progression that takes place, and in each stage, we make decisions that either lead us into immorality or that enable us to have victory of sin. This identifiable process includes the following:

- thoughts
- thoughts produce emotions
- emotions lead to actions

Every temptation starts in your mind. The battle is won or lost in your mind.

"Let no one say when he is tempted, 'I am being tempted by God'; for God cannot be tempted by evil, and He Himself does not tempt anyone. But each one is tempted when he is carried away and enticed by his own lust. Then when lust has conceived, it gives birth to sin; and when sin is accomplished, it brings forth death" (Jas 1:13-15, NASB).

James, the brother of Jesus, writes the stages for temptation; there is a progression that takes place. A process that starts with our thoughts and flows to our emotions. The decisions we make can lead us into the beginning stages of immorality. Temptation is not sin, but if we allow the passions in the progression to keep moving us along, and we act on it, it turns in to sin. In the last chapter, Andrew seeing the nudity on the billboard was nothing that anyone could do to stop it, because it was there. But if we act upon it, and those emotions begin to get stirred and we begin to act upon them, it becomes sin. That's why we must be careful to guard our heart. Guarding our thoughts is vital because our life is shaped by them.

"Be careful how you think, your life is shaped by your thoughts" (Prov 4:23, NCV).

Stages of Temptation

Stage 1: The Look

James says, "when he is drawn away" (1:14) When you are drawn away, the enemy of your soul uses an enticement to bait you, some vulnerability he's working on. Ask yourself, *what and when are the times I am more vulnerable for the enemy to tempt me? Is it when I'm exhausted or discouraged? Is it after my spiritual highs?* Remember, your intimacy is linked to your spirituality and in climates that are spiritually high. The enemy often comes in right after those times with temptation to try to take away that which has been gained spiritually.

Are you more enticed when you're lonely? Are you more vulnerable when you feel hurt or wounded? Has your spouse said or done something that offended you? Are you frustrated or bored, or find yourself drifting? You may be enticed by the look.

Television and movies have gotten us to a place that our resistance to sin has been lowered and we glamorize it. The belief that everyone's doing it has normalized the immorality, passions, and sexual sins. Television and movies never show you the consequences of what comes from that sexual activity. You laugh and joke about it because it's "normal," but it becomes something you find yourself giving in to.

The psalmist prays "Keep me from paying attention to what is worthless" (Ps 119:37, GN). He also says, "I will refuse to look at anything vile and vulgar" (Ps 101:3, NLT).

Action Step: Draw back instantly when you sense you've been drawn away! If you will learn to unmask the patterns of temptation, you will be able to put boundaries and learn to "flee."

Stage 2: The Lust

James says the next step takes place when the look begins to turn to lust: "… when he is carried away and enticed by his own lust" (1:14). We are drawn away by our own desires, the craving of the sinful nature. The enemy will bait you based on your temptation. Do not give the enemy a foothold by sitting in that place where you will be tempted. When you learn to recognize the kinds of situations that tempt you, you will learn through spiritual maturity the way of escape.

Many have not learned to discipline their desires. Doing so is a mark of spiritual maturity, as Paul observes: "Be careful. If you're thinking, 'Oh, I'd never behave like that'—let this be a warning to you. For you too may fall into sin" (1 Cor 10:12, TLB). Stay alert and ask for wisdom to know the early warning signs of temptation so you can bail out early. The warning is clear: Be Alert! Be Wise! Be Aware!

Action Step: Consciously recognize that every temptation can only tempt because of my personal desire.

Stage 3: The Lure

James says, "and enticed. Then…" (1:14). Winning the battle is knowing:

- When am I tempted?
- Where am I when I'm tempted?
- Who is with me when I'm tempted?
- How am I feeling when I'm tempted?

Training yourself to avoid situations that lead to temptation is establishing protective guidelines. Proverbs 4:27 says, "plan carefully what you will do."

The Bible is clear that we must have practical standards that help protect us. Paul reiterates this in Ephesians 5:3, saying, "But among you there must not even be a hint of sexual immorality." No *hint* of impurity. When I was growing up, preachers would say, "no appearance of evil."

One way we do this at CLC for our pastors is that we have a policy for our staff and our pastors that they don't ride in vehicles with someone of the opposite sex alone because of the appearance of evil. We don't go out and eat alone. If I am meeting with women on staff, the door is open. These boundaries protect us. We don't want situations that would give a hint of evil in any way, so we set up practical standards and guidelines. The Bible tells us to flee from evil, and the enemy will leave. These types of standards can be set up for your personal lives also. When you develop personal convictions in the area of your sexuality, it will enable you to guard your heart and life.

Action Step: Quench improper desire by stopping all internal enticements and fleeing external enticements. This is what Paul would say in 2 Corinthians 10:5, "Take every thought captive." If you will learn to refocus your thoughts, attention, you will learn to be victorious.

Stage 4: The Conception

James continues, "when desire has conceived" (1:15). If you don't stop, desire begins to conceive, and the emotion turns to thought. Now when you desire it, you're drawn away by your own lust.

For example, you grab your phone and decide you're going to surf a site because there's a desire and emotion that leads you now to pornography. Now you've made a decision that you will search the sights. It puts you in a dark place in your head where no one will see, and you begin to think about how you will act upon it. Now evil is overcoming you. You're giving in instead of taking every thought captive, and it's pulling you along.

How we win this battle is to decide ahead of time that we're not going to do this. For example, if you struggle with pornography, you buy an app and give a trusted individual—your spouse or someone who's close to you—the password that will tell them if you've gone into a site that's pornographic. You put it on all your devices, to make sure there are guardrails. What you're doing is protecting your own heart and guarding yourself by deciding ahead of time that you're not going to go there. You're giving yourself a good reason to say, "I'm going to stop this before it goes too far."

Action Step: Pre-decide (i.e., ahead of time) not to sin. Never permit yourself to think of one good reason to commit the sin, and you'll never make the choice to sin.

Stage 5: The Birth

James says, "it gives birth to sin" (1:15). The emotions lead to our thoughts and lust, and now we act upon it.

One can see this in the life of King David. In the cool of the evening, David looks out across his terrace and sees the beautiful Bathsheba. She was young, lovely, and bathing. Seeing her wasn't the sin. The sin took place when he continued to look upon her, lust filled his heart, and he desired her. He could have still taken the thought captive and repented, but he determined to commit adultery with her and called for her. This act of sin led to other sins that destroyed many lives. The consequences of sin are not always easy to ignore. They can cause much pain and hurt. David could have stopped all the pain and consequences of his actions if he would have only recognized the stages of temptation he was giving into.

Action Step: Slam on the brakes! If you are on your way to commit the sin, force yourself to submit to the conviction of the Holy Spirit, and abort the sin before it's too late. Don't let the enemy convince you that you can't stop. You can! You have a free will and have the ability by the Holy Spirit. Pray that God will enable you to find the "way of escape" (1 Cor 10:13) in your own heart. Speak the truth of God's Word over your life; get "out of the dark" and into the "light" and that will set you free.

Stage 6: The Growth

James says, "and sin, when it is full-grown" (1:15). If you don't repent, sin begins to become full grown; it grows when sin leads to another sin, and the best thing you can do is step back and magnify the consequences of that sin. If you're married, magnify the consequences of that adulterous relationship. If you're having an attraction toward someone of the same sex, slam the brakes, get support, get into some setting that can help you walk through the emotions because you can overcome it. If you're a single person having a relationship with someone who's not your spouse, magnify the consequences so you can see the price tag for all those involved. Ask the Lord before the temptation to magnify the cost and consequences of the sin. When you realize the cost, it enables you to overcome by the power of the Spirit.

Pastors who have not followed this advice have ruined their marriage, impacted their children, hurt their friendships, and destroyed their ministry. The problem with ministry is that your work is linked to your livelihood. If you give in, all of a sudden everything collapses. We try to encourage ministers to magnify the consequences, because those few moments of gratification will never equal the magnification of the reality of the consequences that you're going to face. Don't throw away your future for a single moment of pleasure!

"[Immorality] may cost you your life" (Prov 6:26, NCV).

Hollywood can make immorality sensational and can glamorize it, but rarely will a movie show how sin destroys lives. Reality shows portray everything as pleasure; if it feels good, do it. Whatever you want to do is fine. As believers, we find ourselves being drawn in. We need to be aware and strive to stay sexually pure.

Action Step: Wake up — Every sin you commit digs your grave: never believe for a moment the lie, "Just let me sin this one more time," as every sin strengthens itself against you for the next time. I encourage all to not walk alone. Allow others into your journey, so you can keep your temptations in the light. It's easier to say, and harder to do.

Stage 7: The Death

James says, "brings forth death" (1:15). There is a separation that brings spiritual death, but God can help you to overcome.

Action Step: honestly cry out to Jesus — regardless of the degree of bondage you are under, the work of Christ is sufficient to set you completely free.

To fight this battle, we must commit ourselves to let God work in us and obediently follow God's standard. I must determine that I will maintain my purity. The following is a prayer that can be used or adapted in this area:

> I'm going to fight this battle of purity. I'm going to guard my eyes. I'm going to guard my heart. I'm going to guard my emotions, and I'm determined that I'm going to walk away. I'm going to renounce it and pray that every bondage, every stronghold, every addiction is broken, in the name of Jesus. I pray every addiction of pornography is broken. I pray every area of immorality be broken today. Let there be a determination today to say, God, I'm walking away. I'm going to fight this fight. I want to be what you have called me to be. Help me learn how to replace and refocus my mind to live morally pure, so I can honor you.

David's prayer of repentance after he was confronted by Nathan is found in Psalm 51.

> Have mercy on me, O God, because of your unfailing love. Because of your great compassion, blot out the stain of my sins. Wash me clean from my guilt. Purify me from my sin. For I recognize my rebellion; it haunts me day and night. Against you, and you alone, have I sinned; I have done what is evil in your sight. You will be proved right in what you say, and your judgment against me is just. For I was born a sinner—yes, from the moment my mother conceived me. But you desire honesty from the womb, teaching me wisdom even there. Purify me from my sins, and I will be clean; wash me, and I will be whiter than snow. Oh, give me back my joy again; you have broken me—now let me rejoice. Don't keep looking at my sins. Remove the stain of my guilt. Create in me a clean heart, O God. Renew a loyal spirit within me (vv. 1-10, NLT).

Most importantly, *do this now!* Don't delay. Take action and commit to come back to God. Do whatever it takes to determine you will maintain your purity before the Lord.

Be encouraged, God has promised to be there as you seek Him.

"Remember that the temptations that come into your life are no different from what others experience. And God is faithful … When you are tempted, he will show you a way out so that you will not give in to it" (1 Cor 10:13).

Chapter 6

Unity of the Church

As we look at how we are to walk out God's commandment to love, we see five areas listed in Galatians 5 that focus on our relationship with one another. The battle with the flesh includes hostility, quarreling, outbursts of anger, dissension and division. Paul reminds us there is an importance to the unity of the Body of Christ.

The Importance of Unity

The mission of Christ is won through unity. When we are unified, there is a release of the anointing of God as the Spirit of God fills our hearts, and we begin to fulfill the work in the ministry of Christ. This passage again deals with the struggle between the works of the flesh and the Holy Spirit guiding our lives:

> So I say, let the Holy Spirit guide your lives. Then you won't be doing what your sinful nature craves. The sinful nature wants to do evil, which is just the opposite of what the Spirit wants. And the Spirit gives us desires that are the opposite of what the sinful nature desires. These two forces are constantly fighting each other, so you are not free to carry out your good intentions. When you follow the desires of your sinful nature, the results are very clear: idolatry, sorcery, hostility, quarreling, jealousy, outbursts of anger, selfish ambition, dissension, division … (Gal 5:16-17, 19-20, NLT).

We know that the Holy Spirit the third person of the Godhead: God the Father, God the Son, and God the Spirit. In understanding the

Godhead, we know He is a God of love. Scripture tells us that God wants us to love one another. Jesus himself gave that command: "So now I am giving you a new commandment: Love each other. Just as I have loved you, you should love each other. Your love for one another will prove to the world that you are my disciples (John 13:34-35, NLT).

Jesus tells us that a new commandment, which will override the old commandment of "love your neighbor as yourself," is to love others as Christ *has* loved us. When we do, our love for one another will prove to the world that we are His disciples. Are we committed to take Christ at His word, and love one another, not in our limited human capacity, but as Christ loves each of us? The Church gets it right when it comes to loving God and worshiping and walking with God. But where we get it wrong is loving one another the way Jesus loves us. Our unity displayed by our love for one another is a witness to the world. It stands as a declaration to the world that Jesus loves them, and that because of His love for them, we love them. That love becomes the very force that releases an anointing through us.

Love one another as Christ loves us.

The Church in Corinth had a lot of issues similar to many we face today. The first thing Paul talks to them about is relationships. Their relationships in the church were broken, resulting in division and dissension taking place. Accusations flew; envy, grumbling and complaining all took place. To resolve these problems, the elders decided to send a letter to Paul, who had planted the church. He writes back:

> I appeal to you, brothers, in the name of our Lord Jesus Christ, that all of you agree with one another so that there may be no divisions among you and that you may be perfectly united in mind and thought. My brothers, some

from Chloe's household have informed me that there are quarrels among you (1 Cor 1:10-11).

Paul's plea is for unity in love and grace. We must stay unified because if we destroy the unity and harmony of the Church, that disunity begins to destroy the family of God. The original translation has the meaning of "no splits or division among you can be represented by a piece of fabric." This fabric makes up the body of Christ, as we are woven together to be a part it. He says let there be no division among you. An illustration of the meaning of the word *division* is taking a cloth and ripping it. As it rips, there is a division and a separation taking place. Metaphorically, Paul says to let there be no splits. Let there be no attacks, grumbling, or gossip, which was a serious problem.

One of the challenges we face today is that churches exist all around us. Sometimes we forget that God has given these principles to the local body as well as the church as a whole.

In 1 Corinthians, Paul asks rhetorically, "Is Christ divided?" (1:13). No, and so neither should His body be. The mission of Christ is one purpose, and when we walk in unity, we win the battle as the body of Christ. A release of the anointing of God takes place as the Spirit of God fills our hearts and we begin to fulfill the work in the ministry of Christ.

Unity requires that the people of God place emphasis on their attitude. As we grow in our relationship with Christ, and have the character of Christ in us, we will intentionally put on the fruit of the Spirit and thus reflect the *nature* of Christ. As we walk in step with the Spirit, we reflect the *mind* of Christ. As we move forward in purpose, we dress in the armor of God, so that we can carry out the *mission* of Christ. If we are truly in Christ and Christ is in us, there will be no divisions among us. Just as Paul told the Corinthians, we are perfectly united in mind and thought.

When division exists, someone has gotten out of step with the Spirit. This misstep or split that occurs isn't just about church doctrine. In fact, usually what splits the church is not doctrine, but methodology. God has called us as believers to encourage one another on the journey and remain intentional in our purpose. If we don't stay focused, the enemy can get a foothold, resulting in division. Paul tells us in his letter to the Ephesian Church to prevent this from happening: "Make every effort to keep the unity of the Spirit through the bonds of peace" (Eph 4:3).

One of the things I have seen through the years as a pastor and being around churches is that the enemy, Satan himself, tries to destroy the work of Christ. He does everything he can to stop the advancement of the kingdom of God in your heart, your family, your city, and around the world. One of the primary tools he uses involves creating dissension within the body. I have learned that dissension, contention, and confusion in the body of Christ does not have to make sense. If the enemy can come in and create doubt and suspicion, and we begin to question the motives of others and separate from them in our hearts, the bond of peace begins to break. The enemy is creating confusion and dissension, which begins to hinder the work of God.

When a church is moving forward and making an impact, or you are moving closer to your family, the enemy is waiting. When you are pressing into God, the enemy is crouching, and he's waiting to bring dissension. If he can get you and your spouse at odds and bring confusion and chaos in your family, that will slow down what God wants to do. A church that has an anointing on it, moving out and making a major spiritual impact, seeing souls saved, miracles happening, and breakthrough taking place as a city turns upside down (or, you could say, right side up) for God—the enemy will want to destroy such a church. He is there to bring division and confusion. That's why Paul would say to us, "Guard and watch over the unity of the church." A church making an impact for the kingdom of God can get paralyzed and neutralized if we don't stay aware of what dissension and disunity can do to the church. When God sees disunity in the body of Christ, that breaks His heart.

God says in Ephesians 2 that we must step up to our responsibility as believers to protect the unity of where we worship and the unity of what God wants to do. Scripture shows over and over that dissention and disunity is a sin. We are agents of unity, and when we walk in unity, an anointing takes place. We have been commissioned by Christ to promote and preserve the "bonds of peace" among believers.

How to Grow in Unity

The best way to be unified as a church is first to maintain an attitude of acceptance. Romans 14 is a classic passage on accepting other believers in the family of God: "Accept him whose faith is weak, without passing judgment on disputable matters" (Rom 14:1).

Paul tells us to maintain an attitude of acceptance especially on disputable matters. He addresses some of the issues in the Early Church. For example, Jewish believers ate certain things and not others as part of their rituals. Non-Jews, called Gentiles, were giving their lives to the Lord and coming to the faith. The Jewish believers with their various customs said that to follow Christ, you must follow certain customs and ways. They began to put this on the non-Jewish believers. Paul continues in Romans 14,

> Let us therefore make every effort to do what leads to peace and to mutual edification. Do not destroy the work of God for the sake of food. All food is clean, but it is wrong for a man to eat anything that causes someone else to stumble. It is better not to eat meat or drink wine or to do anything else that will cause your brother to fall. So whatever you believe about these things keep between yourself and God. Blessed

is the man who does not condemn himself by what he approves (vv. 19-22).

Paul tells them (and consequently us) not to make major issues out of minor things regarding how we should live and what we should do.

Don't major on minors. Paul is saying, don't quarrel about issues that are matters of opinion (disputable matters).

Don't let there be quarrels about issues that are matters of opinion; these are disputable matters. They don't need to cause division among you. If a certain matter is not essential, it becomes a disputable matter. If it's essential, we discuss it, process it, and pray about it. We fast, look into God's Word, and turn to spiritual leaders who can guide and inform us in that essential matter.

Christian Life Center is part of the fellowship of the Assemblies of God. It is not a denomination in that there are rules and regulations that they force or impose on us but a cooperative fellowship that we are a part of—and the largest Pentecostal Movement around the world, located in 260 nations. There are approximately 644 million Pentecostal believers around the world. The Assemblies of God has partners with other Pentecostal Movements that are often called something other than Assemblies of God, be it the Pentecostal Movement or the Pentecostal Union, Pentecostal Fellowship, etc., but they are a part of the World Pentecostal Fellowship. Here in America, the Assemblies of God has almost 13,000 Assemblies of God churches. There are eighteen Bible colleges/universities and a seminary that are teaching and training our ministers in the Word of God.

I got into a program in the movement, which led to my attending a Bible college and later seminary so I could learn God's Word. I could understand who God is and the ways of God and the movement of God. I went as a missionary to Europe, working with the Assemblies of God and believers in other nations to begin to learn how God is moving among different people groups, such as Nigerians, Filipinos, and those from various Asian, African, and Caribbean countries. I began to see the hand of God moving around the world.

The beautiful thing the Assemblies of God does for us is to bring together what's called the Commission on Doctrines and Practices. When there are doctrinal challenges, they bring together theologians and Bible professors who begin to wrestle with these questions and issues. That helps you and I, as members of an Assemblies of God church, to know that we are walking in a theology and doctrine that has been tested and proven around the world. There are 644 million Pentecostal believers, and Bible schools and theologians that help you and I know how to live our lives, according to the Word of God.

> Differences should not be feared or avoided but accepted and handled in love.

On the tough issues of Scripture, if you ever go to the Assemblies of God website, they have what they call position papers that bring clarification to the more complicated issues of our time. It is loaded with Scriptures to help you wrestle with what God says—for example, issues essential on the topic of women in ministry, issues related to the AG position on homosexuality or other issues of morality. All of these different positional papers can help you begin to understand what we believe and how to address essential matters.

However, when it comes to *disputable* matters, Paul says "accept one another." Don't let those types of issues bring division among you.

People will have differences of opinion in the church such as worship styles, dress codes, ministry methods, or doctrinal beliefs about the Second Coming, prophecy, and other things. These are the disputable matters to which Paul refers.

We won't agree on every topic, but we must maintain an attitude of acceptance. We can determine to grow together and move forward in unity.

Chapter 7

Growing in Unity

> Let there be real harmony so that there won't be splits in the church. I plead with you to be of one mind, united in thought and purpose (1 Cor 1:10, TLB).

Over in the Book of Acts, we read that the New Testament Church was in "one accord" (4:24, 5:12). How did they grow in unity? Acts 2 says that one of the reasons they were in one accord is because they were filled with the Holy Spirit, the Spirit led and guided them, and they had all things in common. In the first five chapters of the Book of Acts, ten times it talks about them being unified. It describes them with these phrases: being in one accord; they had one heart; they were together; they were bound; they had one purpose; one mind; one spirit; one soul. If we as the church body will develop the unity of the believers in the Book of Acts, we can have the same power and anointing they did. If we walk in unity, we will see the growth they saw, too.

Not long ago I was working with another church, and the pastor mentioned that they hadn't grown in a long time. While I was there, I could see that they would not experience growth because they didn't know their purpose. They didn't know what they were about or where they were going, and there was no vision. They came together for services, but a healthy church requires more than just a worship service. They must understand their purpose. A church's purpose builds morale and reduces frustration. It allows the people to concentrate and focus and being intentional. It attracts others to join them because they know where they're going as they grow in God together. A church like that is determined to make a major spiritual impact sharing the gospel as messengers of hope.

People become disillusioned with the Church for many understandable reasons, such as conflict, hurt, hypocrisy, neglect, pettiness, legalism, and other sins. The key to unity in the Early Church was their infilling with the Holy Spirit. That gave them courage, boldness, confidence, insight, greater love, and a desire to walk in the fruit of the Spirit. They embraced the mission of Christ to fulfil the purpose of God.

Instead of running away to look for another church, we need to try to reconcile.

Luke tells us in Acts 2:42ff that everyone was loving God. They were in awe of the wonders of God. They felt excitement about God. They came together with "glad and sincere hearts." They committed to spiritual growth, longing to be more like Christ and grow in His nature and character. Learning to die to self and live *in* Christ, they served one another with spiritual gifts. Scripture tells us that God was working in their midst evidenced by salvations, miracles, and life change. As Acts 17:6 says, "they turned the world upside down." That's the power of unity! It's unstoppable what God can do through a unified church.

Too many churches are weak and ineffective because members have gotten offended and don't strive to walk in unity but rather in artificial harmony. Rather than being shocked and surprised, we must remember that the church is made up of people on a spiritual journey. Sometimes—intentionally or unintentionally—we say or do things that hurt each other. No church is perfect. Instead of running away to look for another church, we need to try to reconcile. This can lead to stronger character and deeper fellowship. God has things He wants to teach you, and others as well. This is another way to grow in unity.

The problem with going from one church to another, whether out of disagreement or frustration—or because you just want to church hop based on how you feel that day—is that you're never going to grow and draw the nutrients of what God wants in your life to the point that you will see the spiritual growth of fruit in your life. Spiritual maturity is seen in remaining planted. As we get planted, we begin to bear fruit.

What I see happening all the time is that people don't like the worship service. They don't like what's going on in the ministry. Here they are, they're planted and starting to grow. They're starting to show some fruit, but then they decide they don't like it. They had been accepted, knew their gifts, and were growing in them. They knew the body and the leadership, but for whatever reason, they decide to go get involved in another church, to get planted somewhere else. The problem is, they're not really planted. There's no depth because their roots were not established.

Or maybe they were at the first church being nurtured, the pastors were planting them and helping them till up the soil of their Christian walk and helping them find their gifts. Then just when they really start to get rooted, someone says something or something happens, and they get offended. As soon as they get offended, what do they do? Go to another church.

Now, they might have been here for five years and were just at a point of starting to grow some fruit. Sometimes fruit comes quicker, sometimes it takes longer because God is developing you as He weaves you into the fabric of a church body. He's seeing your gifts and how they benefit the rest of the people in the house. There is something for everybody in the house to grow and to build and encourage one another. It just takes time.

> If you keep uprooting yourself, you'll never grow deep enough.

I believe there's fruit on every tree, and it's coming even if it's not showing yet. But you must remain planted. The problem with too many believers is they don't give enough time for their roots to grow deep. If you keep uprooting yourself, you'll never grow deep enough. You'll never get to the place where fruit can be seen from your life. That's the purpose God has for you. We must know where we're going in mission and in purpose.

I may not be your pastor but let me be pastoral: long to be filled and led by the Spirit. When you walk in the Spirit, you will receive this same courage, boldness, and confidence. God will anoint you, and you will be able to show others a greater love. Walking in the Spirit will empower you to fulfill the mission of Christ, and the church will see God's glory released.

Churches need to become the voice in the city God has called them to be. Christian Life Center desires to be a big voice in a big city, to make a greater impact for the Kingdom. A body of believers unified is unstoppable.

Encouragement through Unity

This common purpose is a choice to encourage and build one another up rather than tear down. We do this by filtering what we say and how we say it. The Apostle James instructs believers on that point: "Dear brothers, don't be too eager to tell others their faults, for we all make many mistakes" (Jas 3:1, TLB).

Remember, the enemy is the accuser of the brethren, not you and me. The enemy brings guilt, shame, and condemnation. You and I should encourage and build one another up. As Ephesians 4:29 says, "Do not let any unwholesome talk come out of your mouth but only what is helpful for building up others according to their needs."

We must refuse to gossip.

This means we must refuse to gossip. What is gossip? A simple definition we use is that gossip is when you're sharing a problem or criticism with someone who is neither part of the problem nor part of the solution. If they're part of the solution, then it's legitimate to share it with them. But if they're not, then it's gossip. Let's be honest, this is hard. We desire to know, and we want to share with others, especially when we have been offended or hurt. Some people when they have a problem with someone else in the church don't go to that person but to everyone else. But, when we do this, it breaks our unity and our anointing.

We need to practice God's method of conflict resolution, and it's found in Matthew chapter 18. If there is some kind of conflict and someone offends you, God lays out a simple plan to follow. If a believer hurts you—whether intentionally or unintentionally—go and tell that person and work it out between the two of you. If he or she listens, you have won a friend. If they won't listen, then take one or two others along so that in the presence of witnesses, you can keep things honest and try again. If they still won't listen, tell the leaders of the church: a group leader, a lay minister, or one of the pastors. If they won't listen to the leaders of the church, then you must confront the individual with the need for repentance and offer God's forgiveness. Private confrontation is always the first step. Often, there is a misunderstanding, and something was perceived the wrong way. When you begin to talk about it, unity is created. In uniting with one another, our roots begin to grow. As our roots begin to grow, we begin to see fruit come from our tree.

Without unity, we as a church will lose our stability. Each of us needs to do our part to protect the unity of the church. If we lose our unity, we lose our voice. May God help us to see the impact He desires to make through us. Our job is to link together as the body of Christ to encourage and inspire to build up one another and glorify God.

Chapter 8

The Deceitfulness of Selfish Ambition

> "Do nothing out of selfish ambition
> or vain conceit" (Phil 2:3-4)

As we work together toward growing ourselves and encouraging one another, we have an overall goal and purpose we'd like to achieve.

In Galatians 5:20, Paul mentions the topic of selfish ambition. Ambition is an earnest desire for some type of achievement or distinction, such as power, honor, fame, or wealth, and the willingness to strive for its attainment. It is a strong desire to do or achieve something, typically requiring determination and hard work; a desire and determination to achieve success.

Ambition in itself is not wrong as this desire leads one to have goals, a sense of purpose, and accomplishment that gives meaning in life. We want to teach our children and the younger generation growing up in an age of entitlement that determination and hard work are good character qualities. We can decide to move forward, to better ourselves, and to move toward godly pursuits. If we didn't have ambition, there would be no reason to go to school, study, invent, or advance the Kingdom.

Paul talks about ambition in Scripture ten times. Of those, seven times he refers to an ambition to share the good news about Jesus and to glorify God. Paul would say he was ambitious to preach the gospel, further the kingdom of God, advance the name of Jesus, make the name of Jesus known, and make His name great. These are good, godly ambitions. Paul understood his gifts, his talents, and his education. He also understood that life was not about him but about the kingdom of God. The Lord had changed and transformed his life on the road to Damascus, awakening him and showing him another way—God's way—leading him to pursue His purposes. The other three times Paul talks about ambition deal with selfish ambition.

The Deceitfulness of Selfish Ambition

Selfish ambition is a motivation that elevates me and puts what I want above the interests of everyone else to have more power, honor, fame, or wealth and to never feel content. Selfish ambition keeps driving me to get more, even when that doesn't make sense. On the other hand, God gives a sense of destiny—a pursuit for His will and purpose. That sense draws me toward growing the kingdom of God and fulfilling His purpose. We can call that godly ambition.

Both kinds of ambition lead to the same place, but the deceitfulness is that it can be difficult to distinguish between the two. The deceitfulness of self-seeking and self-serving, looking out for my own interests above the interests of anyone else around me is where I begin to step out of a godly pursuit to go down a road of pride. In that moment, destiny and God's purpose are no longer my real motivation, as pride draws me to do my own thing. It's about me, and I'm never content with where I'm at. If we don't check those attitudes, pride moves to the center of our universe, and we can never attain fulfillment.

To be led by the Spirit, we must learn to recognize selfish ambition, crucify it on the altar of Christ, and allow God's pursuits and His will to drive our life. Ambition can be so deceitful, dangerous, and difficult to recognize. This is why we call it *a battle within*. You see it when individuals begin to brag about their accomplishments and want to be better known in their company, among their friends, or in other social settings. They try to expand their personal influence or prominence so others will look to them. This is especially true with those who try to get as many followers as possible on various social media platforms. What is it that drives them? Their world is wrapped around the comparison to be the very best and to get ahead of everyone else. That attitude leads to pride and the thinking, "I am the one who has achieved it, and I am entitled to that success because of my accomplishments." An inward struggle begins to arise. It's called insecurity, because selfish ambition begins to push you and drive you to where your character cannot sustain you.

> Selfish ambition can be described as the drive to promote oneself or prioritize one's own interests over those of others.

Spiritual maturity is totally different. A godly pursuit has spiritual maturity within it. Spiritual maturity looks to the needs of others. It involves learning to surrender, trust, and depend on God, no matter what is happening in and around me. God's will and purposes will prevail if I surrender my life to Him. Left unchecked, my selfish ambition will drive me in the opposite direction. Even servants of God can become servants of themselves without realizing it, which is why selfish ambition is so deceitful.

Mark 10 shows how selfish ambition can take place in those in ministry. Jesus is at the end of His ministry and on His way to Jerusalem with the disciples for the last time. He will be arrested, beat, spat upon, mocked, and crucified in Jerusalem. On the way, He tries to let the disciples know what will take place at this time. Remember, at this point, Jesus is doing many miracles and at the height of His ministry. We see this as He and His disciples enter Jerusalem on the day we refer to as Palm Sunday when people are cheering, shouting, and celebrating.

The disciples were also pretty popular at that time. They had been with Jesus the entire time and were doing miracles as well. Mark 10 describes their brush with selfish ambition:

> Then James and John, the sons of Zebedee, came over and spoke to him. "Teacher," they said, "we want you to do us a favor." "What is your request?" he asked. They replied, "When you sit on your glorious throne, we want to sit in places of honor next to you, one on your right and the other on your left" (vv. 35-37, NLT).

They were not listening to what Jesus had *just said* about how He was going to suffer and die in order to fulfill His destiny. It was like they were saying, "Yeah, yeah, we know, but can we sit in positions of honor?" They were ambitious for positions.

Their selfish ambition began to rise up, creating division among the disciples. Why did James and John think they deserved these places in positions of honor? It is believed that their father was wealthy, and that the family owned a large fishing business that actually provided fish for the palace. Here are two young men who grew up dealing with an attitude of entitlement because their wealth made them feel as though they deserved these positions. As a result, they reached a point of selfishness. Wealth makes us look at what we have and believe that we need and deserve more—regardless of what's happening to anyone else around us. This becomes the driving factor. Their motive became one of more power, position, and influence.

Selfish ambition is deceitful. It pushes people somewhere that many are not prepared to go, and their character can't keep them there.

Destiny draws you into the purpose of God and advances the Kingdom. The response of Jesus addresses the heart of their motive:

> But Jesus said to them, "You don't know what you are asking! Are you able to drink from the bitter cup of suffering I am about to drink? Are you able to be baptized with the baptism of suffering I must be baptized with?" "Oh yes," they replied, "we are able!" Then Jesus told them, "You will indeed drink from my bitter cup and be baptized with my baptism of suffering" (Mark 10:38-39, NLT).

When God draws you, there's a preparation and a fortitude, where your character is being developed for the place God calls you to. *God* places us in those positions. The struggle to get to a place where God has not destined you for will mean that you will have to fight to stay in that place. Sometimes we're driving to get to a place that spiritually, we don't have the fortitude, spiritual life, spiritual disciplines, or faith to be. We don't have a marriage that can stand up underneath it. We can't stay where we are driving to be if we're not prepared for what God is calling us to be.

If you struggle to get to a place God has not destined for you, you'll have to struggle to stay there.

The higher you go in your life, ministry, and influence, the greater the spiritual warfare. If you have not prepared for that spiritual warfare, you will not make it in the moment when the enemy begins to attack. Bitter suffering comes when you begin to move into the mission of what God has. It's not something we are afraid of. It's something we rejoice in, because God gives us strength to stand up under it, and we have pursued Him. When we stand with Him, all of a sudden God's weight begins to come upon us, helping to undergird us when the enemy begins to attack.

Candi and I were young missionaries when we moved to Hungary and only the second missionary couple to go in. Hungary had just come through fifty-four years of communistic control. Communists thought they could squash the gospel, but the Church was beginning to emerge there. When we first arrived in Hungary, they only had seven pastors in the whole nation. The communists had left, but their mentality was still there. Going to Hungary was not about what we would do there. It was what God was going to do in us. I had come from seminary and became a military candidate chaplain at the age of twenty-three. I was leading a Christian school at the age of twenty-four. I was ordained very young and accelerated very quickly in ministry. I felt the call to go to Hungary, and this is where God began to make sure that my heart, life, and ambitions were all rooted in His plan and purpose.

We needed to dismiss the crowds and look to the individuals.

God started to show me that we needed to dismiss the crowds and look to the individuals. It began with learning the Hungarian language. I had the degrees and accolades to show my knowledge, but they couldn't understand me. As long as they couldn't understand me, I had no influence. I remember coming home one night and reading a letter from a dear saint in one of our supporting churches. She asked about all the salvations, miracles, and all that God is doing on the mission field. As I read, my heart broke because I had just come from the mechanic to get an oil change. Because I didn't speak the language, and he knew I didn't understand what he was saying and what was happening, I knew that I had been taken advantage of and paid a whole month's salary for work they claimed to have done on my car that they probably didn't even do. There was nothing I could do. I went home thinking *I can't even speak to the mechanic. Now I'm reading a letter asking me about all the souls that are being saved*. It was a crushing time, a time of breaking in my life. But praise the Lord that in those times, God was rebuilding and doing His work in and for all of us. Any man or woman of God who will be used greatly by God will have desert experiences. They will have moments when there's a breaking and a crushing because what God wants to resurrect is something for His glory and purpose. All of a sudden, it's not about what *we* think ministry is about, but what *God* wants in our life. It was through that season that the Lord really shared with Candi and I the power of one, that we are one, that we were ministering with the power of one to those God sends. It was not about the crowd, but the individuals God had placed within the congregation. As we pressed into that, we let God give us the passion, vision, and anointing to be servant leaders in the center of His will.

Take another look at what is happening with James and John in Mark 10. Selfish ambition is rising up. Jesus responds by saying that God decides your place of position. Destiny draws you to the place that God is calling you, but it's not about you. It's about God and what God wants to do through you. He's preparing you to be used for His glory. There's a destiny calling in your life. Jesus says,

> "But I have no right to say who will sit on my right or my left. God has prepared those places for the ones he has chosen." When the ten other disciples heard what James and John had asked, they were indignant. So Jesus called them together and said, "You know that the rulers in this world lord it over their people, and officials flaunt their authority over those under them. But among you it will be different. Whoever wants to be a leader among you must be your servant, and whoever wants to be first among you must be the slave of everyone else. For even the Son of Man came not to be served but to serve others and to give his life as a ransom for many" (Mark 10:40-45, NLT).

Remember that God chooses! Destiny draws you to the place that God is calling you. It's not about you, but about Him and His purpose for your life. He prepared you, places you, and uses you.

Chapter 9

Humility

> "Give preference to one another in honor"
> (Rom 12:10, NAS).

Humility is greatly misunderstood. It's not shyness, being timid, weakness, or a lack of confidence. Many think it is a sign of insecurity. However, to walk in humility, you must be very secure. As you lead from that place, your humility does not mean you lack courage; rather, it begins to show up in a way where others are going to get preference and be given responsibility. There is a great self-confidence and high self-esteem within you when you walk in humility. Jesus tells the disciples they will lead in a different way. The ambition of world leaders who are not believers differs from the way you will lead and live. Godly ambition is driving, and as a result, godly pursuit draws you to be a servant leader.

In John 13, Jesus shows what humility looks like when He comes to that Last Supper and begins to wash the disciples' feet. This act was not His responsibility. Based on His status, this job was *way* beneath Him. All authority had been given to Him, yet He was doing that which a servant would do. In the same way, we can overcome selfish ambition by walking in humility.

Growing in Humility

To grow in humility requires learning to give preference to others, allowing them to go first and get the credit, letting others begin to see that they are respected and honored, and having sincere love for them. It's like a symphony. Many different chairs make up the sections in the symphony: first chair, second chair, and so on. It's said that the hardest chair to sit in is the second chair. Everyone wants to be in the first chair, but the hardest instrument is the backup instrument, or to be the second fiddle. In the same way, God is saying that we need to respect and honor others by putting them above our own desires. When we begin to do that, we begin to grow humility in life. As the Apostle Paul instructs,

> Don't push your way to the front ... Put yourself aside, and help others get ahead. Don't be obsessed with getting your own advantage. Forget yourselves long enough to lend a helping hand. Think of yourselves the way Jesus thought of himself. He was God ... but He took on the status of a slave ... an incredibly humbling process. He didn't claim special privileges. Instead, He lived a selfless, obedient life (Phil 2:3-8, MSG).

And James also instructs, "Be quick to listen, slow to speak and slow to become angry" (1:19, NIV).

Preferring others means we let them go first. When you have the position, the authority, and the power, what do you do? It's not what I'm entitled to, but what I will do.

A godly pursuit focuses life on God first, others second, and yourself last. We use the mantra, "me third." As you begin to live this way, you will be filled with the Spirit and begin to see fruit for the kingdom of God.

Learn from Others

A second principle of growing in humility is the practice of learning from other people. The teachable heart and spirit are willing to learn from anyone. All countries and cultures have strengths and weaknesses. Different generations have unique wisdom and experiences to impart. We can learn so much from one another when we stay open to hearing and many times applying the lessons shared.

Are you willing to listen to the suggestions of others? How do you respond to constructive criticism or feedback?

"Conceited people do not like to be corrected and they never ask for advice" (Prov 15:12, GN).

"If you reject criticism, you only harm yourself, but if you listen to correction, you grow in understanding" (Prov 15:32, NLT).

Humble people are always learning because they are open to correction. They know they are not experts on every topic. One of the greatest aspects of humility is to learn from the experiences of others. How do you do this? Ask questions. Doing so serves as a key to leadership and life, as we never stop learning and growing but must stay open and teachable.

Admit When You're Wrong

When was the last time you said you were wrong? Selfish ambition makes us think we are never wrong. There are times when I have made a mistake by having a wrong perception or thought. I may have misjudged someone's motives or actions. In those times, I need to learn to admit when I'm wrong. Many times, we say the words, "I'm sorry, but …" When we do that, we're not really admitting our mistake but making an excuse. Proverbs 28:13 tells us that a man who refuses to admit his mistakes can never succeed, but if he confesses and forsakes his mistakes, he gets another chance.

James gives instruction how to admit our mistakes: "Make this your common practice: Confess your sins to each other and pray for each other so that you can live together whole and healed" (Jas 5:16, MSG). When you do this, you will overcome hurt and offenses and live out of humility, allowing the body of believers to grow together.

Surrender Your Plans to God

We often make plans without consulting God then ask God to bless our plans. Our ideas often drive what we want instead of us asking God what His plan is for that day. When you ask God first, your destiny and God's will begin to draw you.

James describes what can result from humble submission to God's plan: "God opposes everyone who is proud, but He gives grace to everyone who is humble. So surrender to God!" (Jas 4:6-7, CEV).

"God gives grace to everyone who is humble." What favor and blessings! When you surrender your plans to God, He gives you strength, wisdom, perseverance, and patience in your life. Learn to trust Him and depend on Him by walking in obedience to Him. Develop a servant's heart—one of compassion, kindness, meekness and long suffering. As you do, you will grow in humility.

The Apostle Paul agrees: "Give yourselves to God … and surrender your whole being to Him to be used for His righteous purposes" (Rom 6:13, GN)

Those first few years in Hungary served as God's refining time in my life. There, He took away my ambition, taught me to surrender to Him, and helped me center my motivations on what honored Him. It was a season of brokenness, obscurity, and dependence on God. I have come to learn that every child of God willing to allow themselves to grow in humility will walk through a similar process that leads to fruitfulness in the work of the Kingdom.

Chapter 10

The Battle of Envy

> So I say, let the Holy Spirit guide your lives. Then you won't be doing what your sinful nature craves. The sinful nature wants to do evil, which is just the opposite of what the Spirit wants. And the Spirit gives us desires that are the opposite of what the sinful nature desires. These two forces are constantly fighting each other, so you are not free to carry out your good intentions.
>
> When you follow the desires of your sinful nature, the results are very clear: sexual immorality, impurity, lustful pleasures, idolatry, sorcery, hostility, quarreling, jealousy, outbursts of anger, selfish ambition, dissension, division, envy, drunkenness, wild parties, and other sins like these..." (Gal 5:16-17; 19-21).

Paul says there is a battle of jealousy and envy within the heart of every person. James writes that where there is envy, you will find every kind of evil.

Definition of Envy

Envy refers to feeling envious, jealous, resentful, or begrudging of others; it involves coveting, desiring, aspiring to, wishing for, wanting, longing for, or craving what someone else possesses.

The Bible says that envy can make you power-hungry, rude, sarcastic, spiteful, stingy, stubborn, unforgiving, ungrateful, unkind, and vain. It doesn't paint a pretty picture of what can happen to the body and mind of the one with envy, jealousy, or of the one who covets.

Proverbs 14:30 (NLT) says that "A peaceful heart leads to a healthy body; jealousy [envy] is like cancer in the bones."

King Solomon, one of the richest people who ever lived, understood the nature of envy: "I have also learned why people work so hard to succeed: it is because they envy the things their neighbors have" (Eccl 4:4, GNT).

The reality show *American Greed* is an example of these principles at work in a negative way. It shows the dark side of the American dream where money seduces, power corrupts, and the line between right and wrong blurs fast. It presents a world of scams, murder, and greed through real-life stories of how some people will do anything for more. Such behavior results in the destruction of friendships, families, businesses, neighborhoods, and nations.

Definition of Covet

Coveting is the uncontrolled desire to acquire, particularly what belongs to someone else.

The desire to acquire in itself is not bad. God put that desire into His creation. Many desires or ambitions are healthy and normal. For example, God made squirrels and gave them the desire to acquire nuts. He made birds and gave them the desire to acquire straw to build nests. He has filled the world with all kinds of exciting, wonderful, good, desirable things and given humanity the desire to acquire them. That in and of itself is not bad, but anything uncontrolled is a problem. John describes the dangers of uncontrolled desire and how to deal with it:

> Stop loving this evil world and all that it offers you, for when you love these things you show that you do not really love God; for all these worldly things, these evil desires—the craze for sex, the ambition to buy everything that appeals to you, and the pride that comes from wealth and importance—these are not from God. They are from this evil world itself. And this world is fading away, and these evil, forbidden things will go with it, but whoever keeps doing the will of God will live forever (1 John 2:15-17, TLB).

Those passions in the lust of the flesh are the very things that will entrap you. Don't daydream what it would be like to be married to the spouse of that wife or husband. The Bible says our passions of the flesh become our sin.

The problem with envy is that envy or coveting doesn't stay inside but wants to manifest outwardly. It begins to find a way because it starts in the mind and as it fits into our thoughts, we begin to rationalize. As we begin to rationalize, we compromise. Once we compromise, we step into sin. The moment we step into that sin, we bring the enemy into our realm, into our heart, and into the issue. If we don't repent and turn away from it, that sin becomes a bondage and a stronghold, and we begin to drift in our love for and relationship with God.

Biblical Example: David Sees Bathsheba

David's palace was on the southwest side of the Kidron Valley, and on the northwest side of the Valley was where the temple would have been. David would come out and see the glory of his palace, but he would have looked northward to see that God's presence did not have a house or temple, and God drove him to build the plans of the temple.

Scripture tells us that one time, David came out on the terrace of his balcony, and his guard was down. Temptation was heightened, and his flesh and his will to overcome it was lowered. He looked out and saw a beautiful woman named Bathsheba. It wasn't the first look that got him in trouble; he *continued* to gaze upon her. David saw this beautiful woman who was another man's wife. Her husband was an officer in David's military. David, too, should have been out at the battle. Envy, lust, and other temptations usually manifest themselves when we are not where we should be or doing what we should be doing. It often happens at night under the cover of dark.

King David called for Bathsheba, committed adultery with her—some would say that given his power, that it was rape—and she becomes pregnant.

Proverbs 31 is believed to have been written through the influence of Bathsheba. She's talking to men, and she lists all the issues that David had and speaks against them. It's something that she knew within herself was not right. However, in that day, there was a kingly privilege. Kings had total authority that was completely unchecked and uncontrolled. They did what they desired.

David's plan was to act like he was a hero. When he found out that Bathsheba was pregnant, He called her husband, Uriah, from the battlefield. He commends Uriah and praises him for the battle that's taking place. He gets him drunk and encourages him to go be with his wife. But Uriah had too much integrity and honor to go because his comrades were out on the battlefield fighting and risking their lives. So, he slept on the porch. Even drunk Uriah had more integrity than David but still gave honor to the king.

David realized this plan was not going to work, so he decided to send Uriah back to the battlefield and put him on the front line. Without knowing it, Uriah carried his own death sentence with the kingly seal on it. When that seal was there, it was not allowed to be broken in any way. If it was broken and you were the carrier of the orders, you would be murdered. He took the battle plan and gave it to the generals. David had written to put Uriah at the front of the battle, where it was the hottest and most intense. This assured that he would be killed in battle. Once that took place, David could step up to try to cover his sin by becoming the one that takes this poor grieving widow who's pregnant and care for her. David broke four commandments (#10, 6, 7, 9), and it all started with covetousness in his heart when he envied another man's wife.

The commandment was clear: "You shall not covet your neighbor's house; you shall not covet your neighbor's wife, or his male servant, or his female servant, or his ox, or his donkey, or anything that is your neighbor's" (Exod 20:17, ESV).

The passions in our heart and the **lust of the flesh** cannot be hidden. We must allow the Lord to cleanse them to break the bondage of the passions that would drive us and must learn to discipline those desires.

A second category we see is the **lust of the eyes**. The lust of the eyes deals with possessions, or distractions. In the Ten Commandments, these items included another man's ox, donkey, and house. These are things they would have had, and the Israelites were told not to covet. Some of these are not issues today. However, in today's world it could be that new car, sound system, speakers or TV, a new iPhone, the newest PlayStation. What's wrong with your current one? The item will vary for different groups of people, but it's the possessions that drive us. Remember, acquiring in and of itself is not bad, just as ambition is not bad.

A final category is **the pride of life**, seen through position. For example, a couple begins with a starter home. There's nothing wrong with desiring to get a bigger or nicer place. You start with what you can afford, and as you work, save, and invest, you grow in life, and opportunity arises for a different space or other material things. This isn't bad, unless you go into another's house, see what they have, and suddenly start coveting their status or lifestyle. In biblical times the tenth commandment tells us not to covet another's servants. It would be like talking to a businessperson who has increased their productivity, and their position and salary is moving them forward, and you desire what they have.

> God's answer for winning this battle is contentment.

Advertisers understand this and create within us a dissatisfaction in one of these three areas that pushes us to buy (or borrow so we can buy, getting us deeper in debt) as we try to find satisfaction or happiness in these areas. In the New Testament, Timothy addresses the Church regarding these principles:

> Yet true godliness with contentment is itself great wealth. After all, we brought nothing with us when we came into the world, and we can't take anything with us when we leave it. So if we have enough food and clothing, let us be content. But people who long to be rich fall into temptation and are trapped by many foolish and harmful desires that plunge them into ruin and destruction. For the love of money is the root of all kinds of evil. And some people, craving money,

have wandered from the true faith and pierced themselves with many sorrows (1 Tim 6:6-10, NLT).

God's answer for winning this battle is contentment. Being content is not natural or automatic. It is a learned skill we need to practice. The next chapter will show us how.

Chapter 11

How to Be Content

> Yet true godliness with contentment is itself great wealth (1 Tim 6:6).

Keys to Contentment

"We do not dare to classify or compare ourselves ... [it is] not wise" (2 Cor. 10:12).

How do you react when you see somebody with a nicer car? Do you wish you had that, or are you happy for them? How do you react when you see someone with a nicer house or more beautiful furniture? One of the greatest lessons you can learn is to admire without having to acquire. I don't have to own everything to enjoy it. If the only things you enjoy are the things you own, life is going to be miserable.

Why do we compare? In our society the way we keep score is by possessions. We're insecure. We're always looking around to see how we're doing. However, according to God, our wealth doesn't determine our worth.

Hebrews instructs us, "Keep your life free from love of money, and be content with what you have, for he has said, 'I will never leave you nor forsake you.' So we can confidently say, 'The Lord is my helper; I will not fear; what can man do to me?'" (13:5-6, ESV).

The secret of contentment is not in my money or possessions. Therefore, I refuse to compare myself to others.

Rejoice, and Give Thanks in What You Have!

"If God gives a man wealth and property ... he should be grateful and enjoy what he has ... it is a gift from God" (Eccl 5:19, GN).

A second key to learning and growing contentment in your life is to rejoice and give thanks in what you do have. Instead of focusing on what you don't have or what didn't happen, appreciate what God has given you along the way. Others sometimes look at you and wish they had the same thing.

> One of the greatest lessons you can learn is to admire without having to acquire.

"Isn't everything you have and everything you are sheer gifts from God? So what's the point of all this comparing and competing? You already have all you need!" (1 Cor 4:7b-8a, MSG).

The problem is, we don't believe we have all we need. Through advertising, society tries to convince us that we don't have everything we need. They drive our thoughts and behaviors, but Paul reminds us that we must learn to be content. A secret in life is to learn that happiness isn't getting whatever you want but enjoying whatever you have. This is important because the myth of envy is that if you have more, the happier you will be. Happiness is emotional, but joy is in the Lord. When you understand where your joy is, everything changes.

A key to this growth pattern of learning to be content is delayed satisfaction. When the new iPhone comes out, do you really need it?

Do you need the newest PlayStation model? Why do you need that new car? You might have a good reason. Delayed gratification slows you down so you can check and process your motives. Don't get something because you covet it. Don't do it out of selfish ambition. God wants to bless you so you can bless others and be a blessing to the nation.

A mark of maturity is delayed gratification.

God is watching your generosity. If He blesses you with a new job, how are you honoring Him? If He blesses you with a new book or an album, are you sharing with others? Can He trust you with that desire to have more followers or have a greater influence?

If you've been praying for the bigger house and promise God that you will dedicate it to serve others, God will begin to make a way. In return, you need to let it be a place for people to come share life and learn together. Invite people to come eat and have fun together. Use it to bless others.

Release What You Have to Help Others

God doesn't want to bless you just for your own benefit. He wants you to share and help other people with it. He's watching you to see how much you give away.

We've become a society that keeps and hoards stuff. The New Testament encourages us to help others, share, and give to others. A pastor was telling about how God had blessed their life and they moved to a new house. They got a lawn service at their new house, so he didn't have to cut their lawn. He also didn't have to trim the trees and edge anymore. However, all his lawn equipment sat in the garage. One day when he opened the garage and saw all that lawn equipment, the Lord spoke to him, "If you keep it, I'm going to make you use it. Why do you need it? I've blessed you with this lawn service, so bless somebody else with your lawn equipment." The next day, the pastor gave it away. When I release what I have and share with others, I'm learning to be content.

As God blesses you financially, Scripture warns not to be proud of your wealth. Don't think you're better. Don't trust in your money because you can lose it tomorrow. As Paul instructs Timothy,

> Tell those who are rich, not to be proud and not to trust in their money which will soon be gone. Tell them to use their money to do good … to give happily to those in need, always with others whatever God has given them. By doing this they will be storing up real treasure for themselves in heaven—it is the only safe investment for eternity! (1 Tim 6:17-19, TLB).

Refocus on What's Going to Last

What if you're not getting your dream or reaching your goals? What if it seems like things aren't happening? Keep believing and trusting God. He's in control and knows what's best. He sees it all. Continue to build the kingdom of God by sharing with others, and practice being content. As you refocus on what will last for all of eternity, suddenly things will begin to turn in your own life.

Paul tells us that we must "fix our attention, not on the things that are seen, but on things that are unseen. What can be seen lasts only for a time, but what cannot be seen lasts forever" (2 Cor 4:18).

Question: What will last in eternity?
_____

> What can be seen lasts only for a time, but what cannot be seen lasts forever.

_____

Everything you see is temporary. It will eventually begin to decay or rust, wear out or fall apart, until it no longer exists because all possessions are temporary. Ask the Lord to help you keep your attention on those permanent values that last for eternity. Reorganize your life around eternal priorities.

It is possible to be wealthy and not materialistic. Materialism is an attitude. You can be poor and greedy or rich and greedy. You can be poor and content or wealthy and content. It's the *attitude*, not the *amount* God's talking about.

A sign that you're becoming greedy is that you begin looking at others and thinking or saying something is not fair. Why does this person get more possessions? How did they increase their power or position? Suddenly, you obsess over and compare yourself to what someone else has instead of being content. In these times, you need to reflect on eternal values. What's going to happen after you die? Are you creating a lasting impact? What you did with God's gifts here on earth will do some good if you use it in the right way.

A funeral [took place] in Beverly Hills. A wealthy widow who was worth millions ... died and people gathered around the edge of the casket. Somebody said, "It's so sad. She had so much to live for." The person next to her said, "No. She had so much to live on. She had nothing to live for."

Ask God to increase your generosity, so you can give and share. If you need a place to start, begin with tithing. Remember, "There is more happiness in giving than in receiving" (Acts 20:35, GN). As you grow, you can continue to give beyond the tithe. We tend to live tight fisted. God wants you to live open handed, to share with others, and as you do, you will learn to feel content. Make a goal in your own life to increase your generosity—to give and share. Whatever you give in the name of the Lord and share with others, you will never miss being a part of what God is doing. God will always restore and always give you more because you become His channel and have His blessing.

Conclusion

More Than Conquerors

> "So I say, let the Holy Spirit guide your lives. Then you won't be doing what your sinful nature craves. The sinful nature wants to do evil, which is just the opposite of what the Spirit wants. And the Spirit gives us desires that are the opposite of what the sinful nature desires. These two forces are constantly fighting each other, so you are not free to carry out your good intentions" (Gal 5:16-17, NLT).

We have been learning how to defeat this battle of carnality or the sinful nature. We know that our sinful nature fights against what the Spirit wants to do. We are fighting for who's going to sit on the throne of our heart, and we *can* win the fight.

To win from within we need to not just remove some things but replace them with what God has for us. To live as overcomers, we must be filled with and led by the Holy Spirit. How do you walk in the Spirit? How do you stay filled with the Holy Spirit and hearing what God wants to say? As we learn to listen and obey, we can replace the desires of the sinful nature by putting on the fruit of the Spirit.

To overcome the flesh, we need to experience God on a regular basis. As we connect to His family, we grow in knowledge and wisdom. In serving one another, we maintain unity as a body of believers. As we share life together, we learn how to make disciples. By focusing on the vision, we can fulfill the mission of Christ through the anointing of the Holy Spirit and can glorify God.

I pray that you choose to *want* to live for God, to find meaning and purpose in life, and that you would learn to walk with God and be everything He desires. Choose to live for Him, be filled with His Spirit, and obediently walk it out. That walk begins by committing to God. If you have not already, ask Him to come into your heart and to forgive you of your sin. Ask Him to break the power of sin over your life so you can begin to walk victoriously. When you commit to following God, you will become an overcomer!

About the Author

Tom Manning serves as the Senior Pastor of Christian Life Center (CLC), Fort Lauderdale, FL, a church which reaches over 5,000 attendees on a regular basis. CLC currently has five campuses across South Florida/USA, and two partnering churches in the Cayman Islands.

In addition, Tom is World Missions Director for the Peninsular Florida District of the Assemblies of God—a district giving over $20 million to U.S. and world missions annually. He also served as a General Presbyter for the Assemblies of God.

Previously, Tom and his wife, Candi, served as missionaries with the Assemblies of God in Budapest, Hungary, and as Senior Pastors of Vienna Christian Center (VCC) in Austria from 2000-2012. VCC consists of over sixty nationalities, has twelve weekend services in seven different languages, and reaches over 2,500 weekly.

Pastor Tom is a consultant with Church Life Resources, working with hundreds of pastors and churches annually. He completed his Master of Divinity in Church Growth and Renewal, and his Doctor of Ministry (D.Min.) in Church Health and Revitalization through the Assemblies of God Theological Seminary. He has held pastors training seminars and conventions in over twenty five nations.

Tom and Candi have three sons—Jonathan (wife Stephanie), Christopher, and Andrew. They love boating, traveling, and working with pastors and leaders from around the world.

Are you a church leader seeking to ignite growth and bring life to your congregation? Over 80% of churches today face plateau or decline. In **"Creating Transformational Churches,"** Tom Manning shares proven strategies and Spirit-filled insights to help church leaders break through barriers, tackle decline, and create vibrant communities of faith. This book provides:

• A strategic, biblical roadmap for transformation.

• Tools to address "divine urgencies" that restrict growth.

• A comprehensive plan for creating a thriving lifecycle of ministry and discipleship.

INVITE TOM MANNING TO SPEAK AT YOUR CHURCH OR EVENT

As a seasoned leader with a heart for empowering churches globally, including missionary work in Europe and consulting for ministries worldwide, Tom offers inspiring, actionable teaching for leaders and congregations. Whether you're hosting a leadership retreat, church revitalization seminar, or missions event, Tom brings unparalleled insight and a powerful message of transformation.

TRANSFORMATIONAL CHURCH COHORT

The Transformational Church Cohort equips pastors and leaders with biblical principles and practical strategies to address today's challenges and foster thriving congregations.

• **Gain Clarity:** Assess your church's current reality and align with God's mission.

• **Renew Spiritual Vitality:** Rebuild Pentecostal spirituality, cultivate prayer, and inspire worship.

• **Build Strong Leaders:** Identify, train, and empower your team for greater impact.

• **Plan for Growth:** Utilize proven frameworks to drive spiritual and numerical growth.

With experienced consultants and peer collaboration, this program offers tools and insights to reignite your vision and create lasting change.

Learn more at **messengersofhope.com**

Level 1: Character Formation
Build a strong foundation through classes like "Your Character and Truth" and gender-specific studies.

Level 2: Ministry Formation
Develop ministry skills with topics like "The Heart of Ministry" and "Unwrapping the Gifts of the Spirit."

Level 3: Leadership Formation
Step into leadership with insights from "The Law of the Lid" and "What is a Leader?"

CLC Products offer sermon series and discipleship materials that are ready to implement, saving you time and maximizing your ministry's impact.

Sermon Series Bundles
Each sermon series bundle is designed to address real-life challenges while helping your congregation grow in faith and understanding. These bundles include everything you need to deliver powerful messages with ease.

What's Included:
- Sermon notes and outlines
- Sermon recordings
- Graphics and promo materials
- Social media tools

Save time and focus on leading while we provide the tools you need. Our resources address relevant topics that tackle the key challenges your congregation faces today, all crafted with professional quality to elevate your ministry.

Browse these resources now at **messengersofhope.com**

www.ingramcontent.com/pod-product-compliance
Lightning Source LLC
LaVergne TN
LVHW061556070526
838199LV00077B/7067